TUMBLING

FOR STUDENTS AND TEACHERS

By

SAMUEL F. HARBY, M.A.

Formerly of the Department of Physical Education
Columbia University
and the University of Washington

with a Foreword by

Jesse Feiring Williams, M.D.

ILLUSTRATED

PHILADELPHIA AND LONDON

W.B.SAUNDERS COMPANY

1932

MADE IN U. S. A.

PRESS OF
W. B. SAUNDERS COMPANY
PHILADELPHIA

FOREWORD

AMONG the many changes which have taken place in physical education in the last twenty years, none is more remarkable than the marked increase in books dealing with the subject matter of this important phase of education. From a period when there was only Posse's Special Kinesiology of Educational Gymnastics to which students might refer to the present when the book lists contain innumerable titles on physical education, there has taken place a remarkable transformation in content in physical education. The old types have been replaced with newer forms, and with this change has come about an unprecedented extension of physical education throughout the nation.

In enthusiasm for the rapid strides made by the profession we are apt to overlook our weaknesses and shortcomings. In contrast with the older teachers of physical education, many of our present ones seem tremendously lacking in technic. There are methods that are efficient. There are tested procedures. There are ways of organizing teaching and directing activities that have been established in numerous laboratory situations. Too often the emphasis upon play and

11

expressive activities has been made at the expense of efficient teaching procedures. We need at the present time teachers in the freer types of activity who are as well trained, as orderly in their thinking and as systematic in their efforts as the teachers of a previous gymnastic period.

It is a pleasure therefore to introduce to the profession a book that deals with desirable material in a well organized and orderly fashion, and to express the hope that it will aid, as it promises to do, the better teaching of physical education.

JESSE FEIRING WILLIAMS.

PREFACE

THE reader is no doubt acquainted with a number of books on tumbling. A great quantity of material has been written, listing stunts, describing procedures, discussing theories, etc. If he has attempted to learn or teach tumbling, however, without the personal aid of an expert, he probably feels very much as does the present writer who found it necessary to learn most of his tumbling by trial and error. Books were helpful in suggesting stunts, but the method of performance in each case was laboriously worked out. The books available in the past have had their merits, of course; but the writer feels that none has been entirely satisfactory for teaching the reader to actually *perform* stunts.

A long felt need for a book which would provide a thorough analysis and adequate description sufficient to enable performers to learn or instructors to teach tumbling stunts, has stimulated this effort.

The present treatise is the result of fifteen years' experience with the sport. No stunts are described which the author does not perform. Because the experience is first-hand, it should be accurate. The teaching method and technics have been tried with good results at several public schools in Seattle, Washington, and at the University of Washington over a period of years. With experimentation and long usage as a basis, this presentation should, if nothing else, be practical. The writer hopes that you may experience as much pleasure in using it as he has in preparing it.

SAMUEL F. HARBY.

500 RIVERSIDE DRIVE,
  NEW YORK CITY,
    April, 1932.

CONTENTS

TUMBLING FOR
STUDENTS AND TEACHERS

CHAPTER I

RECENT TRENDS IN PHYSICAL EDUCATION

IN the evolutionary scheme of life, our muscular and nervous system developed concomitantly. Nerves seem to have originated as a supplement to muscles for better control. With increased powers of locomotion came new situations and need for greater nervous activity in adjusting to widened environment. So the two systems have gone their way together, each stimulating the development of the other, from the most primitive form to the very complex organization in mankind.

The physical is the foundation for all human activity. Only through the physical organism can the mind express itself. On the other hand mind is master of the body. It is the soul of man. Plato's ideal was "body for the sake of soul." We can subscribe to that but, as Aristotle put it, "We must strive to attain the harmonious balance of all the claims of life." Man possesses the most highly developed nervous system among living creatures. He must not forget, however, that attitudes of mind and function of brain are modified by physical states, that only through the body can concepts of the mind be realized.

Biologically, man has changed very little, if at all, in the last two thousand years.[1] Social evolution has gone ahead rapidly. As a result man, today, with his original equipment faces a difficult problem of adjustment to the environmental setting. Modern industrial life in most cases fails to provide the proper muscular activity to satisfy biologic needs of the organism.

Various systems of physical training have been offered to relieve this difficulty, each growing out of specific needs in a particular situation. In the last century formal gymnastics, of the kind developed in Sweden by Ling and in Prussia by Jahn, held center stage. These grew out of a strong nationalistic movement and served a definite military purpose. The attempt to use them in modern American life is clearly bad. They represent another continent and another century. They are not applicable to our situation. Recent movements in this country have been away from formal gymnastics, and toward the embodiment of the exercises, known to be beneficial, in games and other forms of activity more natural and more pleas-

[1] Osborn, H. F. *The Origin and Evolution of Life*, New York, 1919.

ant to engage in.   The results have included several distinct advantages:

While not losing in the direction of individual body development, we have appealed to a very much larger group.

We have made fun of work, and thereby insured its use.

We have learned to develop certain attitudes, and standards of conduct, in addition to the usual skills, so that physical training now makes a real *educational* contribution.

Thus has been brought about the displacement of the term Physical Training by the more inclusive and more purposeful term, Physical Education.

Physical Education to-day concerns the mind as well as the body, society as well as the individual. It is more than violent muscular contraction. It implies desirable changes in the nervous system that will add to the individual's equipment for living.

The newer Physical Education program, as sponsored by The American Physical Education Association, has the following objectives:[1]

> To develop and maintain the organic systems of the body.
>
> To develop the neuro-muscular systems of the body with respect to fundamental skills.

[1] Williams, J. F.   *Principles of Physical Education*, W. B. Saunders Co., Phila., 1930, pp. 13–19.

To encourage play, recreation.

To develop standards of conduct.

It is an attempt at a more complete adjustment of the individual and society through the medium of organized and directed physical activity.

In the following pages we hope to show how the use of tumbling as a sport is directly in line with this progress, and how it can contribute to each of the purposes set forth as objectives of our program.

CHAPTER II

THE PRACTICAL VALUE OF TUMBLING

To satisfy the biologic needs of the organism we need to run, jump, climb, push, throw, roll—to engage in all sorts of activities and sports that include these primitive exercises. They are the kind of movements used by nature in the evolutionary process to develop the human species. Since they have made man what he is, they are therefore best adapted to maintain maximum functioning of his body.

Tumbling, perhaps as well as any sport, embodies these primitive exercises. It is an activity very close to our animal nature. Visit the zoo, and watch the animals exercising in their cages. Monkeys are perfect acrobats. The bear-cub finds outlet for his abundant activity in rolls and runs, jumps and climbs. The lion keeps fit by pacing back and forth in his small quarters, rearing with each turn, and by going through a definite system of stretching exercises. All these movements are embodied in tumbling. It is a most natural activity.

An individual's functional health is usually the health of his vital organs: heart, lungs, digestive

21

apparatus, nervous structures, etc. Large muscles are not necessarily indicative of healthy organs. But the function of the vital organs is modified and stimulated by the action of the skeletal muscles, especially the muscles of the trunk.[1] These evolved first in the natural state, and are most important. Other things being equal, the most healthful exercises are those that develop the large muscles of the trunk. Tumbling does this to excellent advantage.

Health of vital organs is dependent not only upon the *condition* of the skeletal structures, but upon their *position* as well. Proper position is important to the proper functioning of both muscles and organs. It makes for maximum advantage in movement with minimum effort and assures ample room for the vital organs. We unconsciously associate alertness with good posture, because the well-poised body is alert.

The period of adolescence is the period of greatest growth, and of greatest danger to posture. The long muscles of the back which support the trunk are extensively stretched and weakened. They must be developed equally with those of chest and abdomen. Tumbling is conducive to all-round development.

A good body is one that enables us to meet the demands of our environment. It need not be exceedingly strong, but it should be agile and perfectly

[1] Williams, J. F. *Personal Hygiene Applied*, W. B. Saunders Co., Phila., 1928, pp. 117-29.

controlled.   Agility implies adequate strength; control implies grace.   This combination is unbeatable for the purpose named.   Acrobatics can make a significant contribution toward its attainment.   Such development enables one to better serve both his own ends and those of society, to protect himself, and to better enjoy life.

Tumbling is a sport adaptable to almost any conditions and to most people.   Little equipment is needed, and large numbers can be handled easily.   The variety of program holds interest for boys and girls alike, children and adults.   It should therefore be very useful.   We wonder that it has not been more widely used.   A possible explanation lies in the fact that few people know anything about it.

Tumbling stunts are graded in difficulty.   A simple progression, with no missing links, is afforded.   Any normal person can begin the easy work and progress slowly toward the difficult.   He may go as far up the scale as his capacity allows.   Provided he learns each trick well before going on to the next, and barring indiscretions, there is absolutely no danger.   Supposing a normal physique, all that is needed to make a good tumbler is willingness, practice, and able supervision.

A chapter on values would not be complete without a discussion of educational values.   Dr. John Dewey's statement that "The only true education comes through the stimulation of the child's powers by the demands of the social situations in which he finds himself," leads us to believe that education is *living*, rather than preparation for the future.

We have already pointed out that tumbling embodies the natural primitive exercises. It is very close to the play life of the child. When more than one engage in it, it is a fine socialized experience demanding cooperation, control, dependability, and courage. As one learns it, it becomes a part of his life. In addition, such activity is fun, and the pleasure that attends its performance gives abiding satisfactions which insure repetition. The laws of exercise and effect are fundamental in learning stunts.

Thus we see that tumbling as an activity contributes to each of the four objectives of our Physical Education program:

It nicely develops and maintains the organic systems of the body.

It affords fundamental skills: for daily use, for safety education, for leisure time.

It is joyful recreation.

It develops standards of conduct.

In short, it is a splendid physical educational activity —worthy of more attention than has hitherto been given it.

CHAPTER III

THE AESTHETIC VALUE OF TUMBLING

We have been inclined to overlook the aesthetic phase of our physical education work, especially for men.

Rhythm is essential to all the arts; and the most fundamental form of rhythm is bodily movement. Opportunities for self-expression, for design, for appreciations of artistic effect, in physical education are immense, and—we regret to say—paid little attention. The only branch of sport in which we have definitely recognized aesthetic value is the dance. There are other physical activities rich in aesthetic worth, only we have failed to realize their possibilities.

M. T. H. Sadler, in an essay, *The Value of Eurhythmics To Art*,[1] speaks of a marked tendency in modern artistic theory to break down the barriers that convention has erected between the various arts. The truth is coming to be realized that essential factors of all arts are of the same quality, and that one art differs from another only in method of expression and the condition connected with that method.

[1] Sadler, M. T. H. *The Value of Eurhythmics to Art*, Small Maynard. Boston, 1928, included in the Eurhythmics of Jacques-Dalcroze, p. 61,

Mr. Sadler goes on to say, "This common basis to the arts is not easily defined, but one important element in it—perhaps the only one we can give a name—is rhythm. Rhythm of bodily movement—the dance—is the earliest form of artistic expression known. It is accompanied in nearly every case with rude music, the object being to emphasize the beat and rhythmic movement with sound.

"Words with music soon followed and from these beginnings—probably war-songs or religious chants— came song-poems, and then poetry as we know it to-day. The still more modern development of prose-writing, in the stylistic sense, is merely a step further.

"The development on the other side followed a somewhat similar line. The rhythm of the moving figure was reproduced in rude sculpture and bas-relief, then in painting."[1] Impressionistic and expressionistic design are romantic portrayals of the same reality. They represent the extreme development in this direction.

So we have, as it were, a scale of the arts, with the dance at the center and prose-writing and design at its two extremes. From end to end of the scale runs the unifying thread of rhythm.

It is seen from this figure that there are two kinds of rhythm: rhythm of time, and rhythm of space. Time suggests our inner sense; space, our outer sense: the one spirit, the other body. Time rhythms we interpret

[1] Ibid., pp. 61–64.

Kip off back.

directly by a time-sense; space rhythms we interpret symbolically by a space-sense, which is sight. Human motion gives the convergence of time and space. In art, therefore, it possesses great charm, borrowing from both ends of the scale. Human beings can be arranged in groups as lovely as any painted design, with the added grace of movement.[1]

The dance, as it appears on the professional stage today, is a vivid embodiment of these principles. Dancing as an activity is becoming more popular each year. Unfortunately, however, with the exception of social dancing it is engaged in almost exclusively by women. Men for some strange reason have come to scorn aesthetic dancing as effeminate, and to confine their physical activities to athletic contests. In our modern sports program for men there tends to be a minimum realization of aesthetic opportunities which under different circumstances might have important value for both spectators and performers.

Tumbling is a compromise between strenuous athletic activity and aesthetic dancing. No one can justly accuse the acrobat of being effeminate, yet he has almost as wide a range for artistic expression and appreciation as does the dancer.

The show aspects of tumbling are not its only aesthetic values. The opportunities it offers for self-expression are also important.

[1] Harvey, J. W.   Unpublished.

In this machine age of ours there is little opportunity for self-expression through the usual channel of industry. The ordinary man's work is standardized. Not many years ago under the system of home-industry workers put their souls into their work. Shoes to the cobbler were a means of expression, each pair a work of art. The great majority of us to-day are neither artists nor artisans. We are workers, and that is all. Art has been completely separated from our normal occupational life. If we desire it, we must seek it in our leisure time.

There is a fundamental drive in each of us for self-expression. It is a force crying out from within, that makes men strive for individuality. Expecially in the United States do we emphasize individuality. President Hoover's book, *American Individualism*, acclaims this quality as the foundation of our American life and government.

Bodily expression is older than verbal. It is the most fundamental of all means of expression. The Carnegie Report on American College Athletics[1] indicates that football as we play it today is more work than play, that its healthful effect on the player is very doubtful. Despite this, football is a very popular sport. We never lack players. A partial explanation is that the game offers good opportunity for self-expres-

[1] *Carnegie report on American College Athletics*. Bulletin 23, pp. 106–107.

sion. Most of our sports offer this opportunity, but in varying degrees.

Because of the nature of tumbling—its display qualities and beauty, its great variety affording stunts within the capabilities of everyone, its adaptability to individual or combination work, its infinite number of space and time rhythms, its pleasureableness—the sport lends itself very well to creative work. It gives more stimulus for self-expression than almost any other sport.

Robert Ingersoll said, "The beautiful refines. The perfect in art suggests the perfect in conduct. The harmony in music teaches, without intention, the lesson of proportion in life."

CHAPTER IV

PRELIMINARY INSTRUCTIONS

THIS chapter contains instructions complementary to those given later with the directions for specific stunts. They are set forth to caution the instructor, or performer, to the end of avoiding unnecessary dangers or difficulties.

It is commonly believed that the tumbler is in constant peril of breaking his neck, that each stunt is a new risk, and that he must be a brave fellow indeed to face the hazards. As a matter of fact tumbling, well supervised or prudently practiced, is not hazardous. It need not be more dangerous than the average sport. Certain precautions are necessary.

Until one has become proficient in the performance of a stunt he should never practice it off the mats. Mats are quite important to learning tumbling. It is foolhardy to attempt advanced stunts without this protection. When mats are used, accidents rarely occur. In learning the very difficult work you should use as an extra safeguard a suspended tumbling belt. For elementary stunts, however, the belt tends to be more trouble than help.

32

The order of stunts as set down in this book forms a simple progression from easy to difficult. You will find it best to follow this order. If you master each stunt before going to the next, you should be perfectly safe.

In every stunt where a person jumps or is thrown into the air, someone should stand by to assist in case of need. The trick of "spotting" is very helpful. It is usually employed to aid a person in making air-turns, and consists of striking the person in flight with your hand behind his knees (in the case of back turns), or neck (in the case of forward turns) in such a way as to spin him around to land upright.

Often in companion work it is helpful for the instructor to place a hand on the shoulder of the man to be thrown, thereby steadying him during flight.

In companion work the matter of signals is of great importance. A double count like, "Ready—go!" or "Allez—oop!" is best. The interval of time between first and second signals should be always the same, about two seconds. The topman usually calls signals; and in addition to expressing them verbally, expresses them with motion. For instance, he may rise on his toes, or pull against the grip of the understander as the first or preliminary signal is called, and throw as the second or executory signal is called. The time interval being always the same, the understander knows exactly when to throw after receiving the preliminary

3

signal. This he gets by hearing, touch, sight, or preferably by all three.

It is often necessary to practice the throw or jump before the topman actually takes the turn-over. Even professionals practice the throw much more often than the turn-over. It should be clearly understood by each partner what the other is going to do. When the topman wants only the throw, let him call "Practice" before giving signals. When he wants to complete the stunt let him say, "Right-over." These precautions may seem trivial, but they are of the utmost importance, and will save many falls if rigidly observed.

Carelessness can not be tolerated; and in companion work at least, "horse-play" is entirely out of place.

Tumbling is delightfully attractive. As an activity it is mentally stimulating and satisfying. If skilfully directed it should afford a carry-over interest adequate to assure its existence as an extra-curricular activity in any school. Clubs for tumbling are numerous. It is a self-testing activity, and affords the individual opportunity to try himself out, which we all want to do. With the great variety of stunts, he must surely excel in some one. This excellence, however small, gives genuine satisfaction, and leads to further activity. Practice brings increasing control. Progress is definitely measurable. The individual's pleasure will likely depend upon his skill and progress.

Instructors should be liberal with praise, and encouraging with their criticisms. Criticisms should be simple. A pupil will likely not be able to correct more than one difficulty at a time. The instructor should choose the greatest fault with each attempt at performance by the pupil, and have him strive to overcome that error.

It is better not to over-caution. Very few of these tricks are dangerous. Fear will cause more trouble than over-confidence. All living things have a natural dread of being in unnatural positions. Ease and control when up-side down or falling are hard-won prizes. They come with practice. Confidence is a great help to attaining control. Be brave and daring, but always careful, remembering that "discretion is the better part of valor."

It will be found that all members of a class do not progress alike. Individuals should be allowed to go ahead as fast as they are able. The interest of apt pupils may suffer if they are required to wait for the class. They can, however, be employed to help others. Teaching a stunt to someone else improves surprisingly your own ability to perform it. It makes you focus attention on technics. Also, a demonstration provokes best effort.

Don't be impatient for progress. Remember that proficiency in tumbling represents years of practice. No one can learn over-night. Be satisfied if you are making definite progress, however small, and having fun. All will come in time.

It is necessary to give intense and consistent effort. You must be brave; and you must take the bumps good-humoredly. After a fall, if you are not badly hurt, get up and immediately try again. Never let a fall break your nerve—yet remember to be calm and careful.

Turn-outs should be short, about an hour's duration. In beginning, warm up by doing simple stunts. The first strenuous effort will probably leave you dizzy. You may see little white spots before your eyes. These are natural reactions with everyone, and should cause no concern. As soon as your circulatory system quickens to the pace of your exertion, all will be right.

Once you work up a sweat, keep busy. Don't allow yourself to cool down, until you are ready to stop and take a shower. Better to have short turn-outs and work hard, than long turn-outs and work only half-heartedly.

For keeping in good shape, one practice a day is the maximum, twice a week the minimum requirement. Before a special performance a day's rest is advisable. For public performances it is needless to "warm up." The thrill of being before an audience is usually sufficient to quicken the pace of your circulatory system and render the usual preliminaries unnecessary. A few jumps about in the wings will be adequate.

Tumbling is a strenuous sport and causes profuse perspiration. Always take a shower after your exertion. It is the decent thing to do, and as an hygienic measure is important.

A good tumbling costume will be scant. The less you wear the better. However you should wear at least supporter, pants, shoes, and shirt. The supporter is indispensable, since bumps and strains are inseparable from tumbling. The lighter the shoes the better; but one should not go without shoes for they bind the foot together and protect the arches. Tumbling without shoes often breaks down the transverse arch and spreads the foot. Pants and shirt are a cleanly precaution. Mats are always dirty, so it is not wise to expose too much of your skin to them. Not only are you liable to minor infections from the mats, but you dirty the mats for others. Sleeveless shirts (which leave the arms free for grips), are best.

A little time and effort is always well spent in caring for the mats. If properly cared for good mats will last a life time. They should not be left on the floor for Tom, Dick, and Harry to walk upon. They should be walked upon as little as possible, even by the tumblers. They should be cleaned frequently.

What has been said in this chapter is important as general instruction. You may learn it before putting on your suit. All of what follows is specific, and deals with the separate stunts. Take the book with you into the gymnasium and try what you read. Learn by doing.

CHAPTER V

ELEMENTARY TUMBLING—INDIVIDUAL

THE reader should clearly understand that the stunts of this book are arranged in a progression from easiest to most difficult, each one being described *in detail*. If you have no difficulty performing a specific stunt you will perhaps be bored reading the details. Remember, however, that the description is designed for those who have difficulty performing the stunt. Whenever you are one of these you will appreciate the details; whenever you are not, pray skip over until you find something more helpful.

It is bad literary taste, and perhaps illogical, to use several hundred words describing what actually takes place in one second. We regret having to jeopardize the artistic for the practical, but it seems impossible to avoid such an arrangement in giving a detailed analysis of movements and technics.

THE ROLL

The roll is the simplest of tumbling feats, yet the principles involved are the same as those involved in more difficult tumbling. Learn the roll well and you will be prepared to tackle the other stunts with increased confidence and skill at managing your body. The roll is valuable not only as a stunt in itself, but also as an exercise to develop control. In addition it is useful and at times necessary in finishing off more difficult stunts.

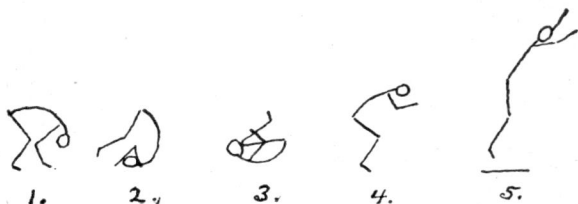

1.   2.   3.   4.   5.

Start from a standing position with your feet about eighteen inches apart. Stoop forward, bending your knees, and place your hands on the mat about eighteen inches ahead of your toes, and as wide apart. The direction of the hands here, as in almost all tumbling stunts, is straight forward. Duck your head forward. (Fig. 1.)

By straightening the knees and pushing with the legs the body weight is thrown forward, and you roll onto your shoulders and the rounded back. The back of the head only should touch the mat, and that very lightly. (Figs. 2 and 3.)

The weight of the body in turning over must fall on the proper muscles. The arms take the weight first, as you enter; it is shifted to the shoulders as you duck your head; and finally to the back, as you roll. The instant you duck your head and the weight goes onto the shoulders relieving the arms, draw yourself up into a tight ball, the *tuck position*. (Fig. 3.)

In the tuck, knees are on chest, slightly separated, head forward and down in between knees; back is rounded, heels drawn in close to buttocks, and hands are on shins just below the knees, arms clasping the legs to the body. We shall have occasions to refer to the tuck later; also to the half-tuck which is a loose ball, or one in which the legs are not fully drawn in.

If your tuck is right the roll will be smooth and you will come nicely out of it onto your feet. If you fail the first trial, consider what you did wrong. Some persons do not duck their heads enough. Others fail to round their backs, or fail to push their weight over properly with the legs. Some do not push equally with both legs, or carry the weight equally on both arms. Such errors usually cause rolling on one shoulder or a collapse. They are easy to correct with practice and attention to directions.

Some persons, who are not used to being upside-down, grow panicky on their first trial. In time, they become accustomed to the inverted position and feel quite at home upside-down. Fear and tumbling are not good partners. Panic is the cause of most accidents. Conquer it at the start. Negative adaptation is the remedy, and may be acquired through practice.

The roll is here described in its simplest form.   If you can execute a roll in this manner, try it in better form.   Bring the feet closer together.   Spring a little as you enter.   Pull your elbows into your side as you turn and point your toes while they are off the mat.   Pointed toes add beauty to any stunt, and bringing the elbows in tightens the muscles of your back to cushion your fall.

The forward roll offers many opportunities for variation.   Following are some suggestions.

Roll without using the arms.

Roll with crossed legs.

Hold your toes throughout.

Roll with arms between legs, hands on outside of ankles.

Roll using only one leg to stand on, arms outstretched at sides.   Get your start by putting one leg out in front, and swinging it back for momentum.   Don't touch this leg, or the hands, to the mat throughout the roll.

Roll over with a half-twist to face downward.

THE DIVE

The so-called dive is merely a forward roll with entrance extended.   Accentuate the spring at the beginning, so that feet leave the floor before hands touch.   The roll enables you to come out of the dive safely.   Don't try to dive very high or a long distance at first. Begin with the simple roll and gradually increase your spring. Increase your distance or height only a little with each trial. Be sure you have perfect control, good form, and do not forget to duck your head at the right moment.

The *take-off*, or jump from the mat, is a very important part of all stunts wherein you leave the floor, *e.g.*, dives, air-turns. The perfect take-off will be described in detail later when we discuss the front somersault. For the time being use any take-off natural to you, preferably one in which you leave the floor from both feet at once. (Fig. 1.)

While you are in the air on the dive straighten your body and hold your head up, with eyes open. Reach well out in front of you for the mat, and keep your body on an "even keel," like a lion springing on his prey (Fig. 2). The feet should fly high so you can fall easily into the roll. The arms receive about one third the shock of falling. You must be prepared to receive this jolt on your arms. If they are too weak to support it, or are unintentionally collapsed, you will receive a bad bump. Since this kind of fall may hurt your neck it must be cautiously avoided.

Remember to use your arms as shock absorbers (Fig. 3).

When your hands touch, duck your head sharply. This must be done in the moment you are holding up with your arms, to protect the head and neck. The roll follows immediately (Fig. 4).

The further you dive the harder it is to hold your tuck, and the worse the bump if you let loose. High dives are harder than long dives, since you hit with a greater thud, and the tendency is to flip over too far. The course of all dives should be up and down. (Fig. 2.) Don't try to dive straight at the mat or to a point ahead. Always dive up. Make your body curve over an arch and down. The caution to keep the feet well up is particularly applicable to long dives. When you make your curve over the peak of a high dive the tendency is for the legs to flip over too far and make you fall too much on your back. In such dives be careful not to let the feet fly too high.

As you come out of the roll onto your feet, finish with a little jump, throwing the arms up. This motion is merely a flourish, since it does not come from the momentum of the roll. But it looks very nice.

BACKWARD ROLL

The backward roll is but little more difficult than the forward roll.

Stand erect with back to the mat. Squat as if to sit on your heels, at the same time falling backward and dropping arms at your sides. The hands are first to touch. They are placed on the mat, fingers pointing forward, about twelve inches behind the heels. The arms bear a third of the shock of falling. The buttocks touch next about six inches behind the hands. Be sure that you sit not more than eighteen inches behind your heels. This means that knees must be bent. Heels,

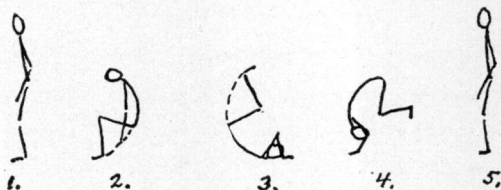

1.   2.   3.   4.   5.

hands, and buttocks are three points on an arc extending the curve of your back (see diagram). Consequently if this arc is preserved during the fall you will rock up on the back of your neck, almost over, without an effort and with only the force of the fall. When you are on your back shift the hands from their first position on the mat to points behind the shoulders. When the feet get to the top of their swing kick them over the head, straightening the back a little, and push with the arms. This will roll you completely over and bring you onto your feet.

The momentum resulting from the first roll is sufficient to carry you into the next, so it is not necessary to assume the upright position between each roll. Just continue smoothly from one to another.

Be careful not to sit back too far away from your heels on entering the roll; not to kick before you reach the peak of your rocking swing; and not to straighten out your body (from the half-tuck position) at any time. Don't forget to use the arms both on sitting down and on pushing over from the inverted position.

HEADSTAND

This stunt is quite simple if you stop to figure it out. It is a lesson in physics as much as coordination.

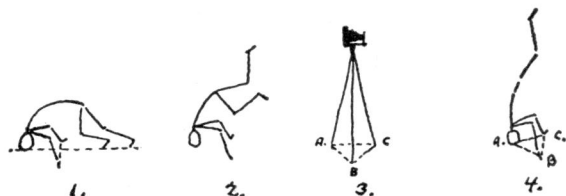

Stand erect at the edge of the mat with left foot about twelve inches ahead of the right. Place the hands on a line about twelve inches ahead of the forward foot and about eighteen inches apart. It will be better for the fingers to point out to the side, rather than straight forward as usual (Fig. 1).

Kick the right or back foot up toward the erect, inverted position, following immediately with the left or forward foot (Fig. 2). It will probably be easier to take the first balance with hips and knees bent, and back slightly rounded. When you've stood like this, try straightening the body. The more rigid and straight you are the easier it will be to balance.

You have three points on which to base your stand, like a tripod. They are head, right, and left hand. If these three points are placed equidistant, and the body is held rigid with its center of mass directly over this base, the whole structure cannot help but stand. (Figs. 3 and 4.) The usual error is to place the hands nearly on a line with the head, instead of back on a line at least a foot away from the head. You know what happens to your camera tripod when you place the legs nearly on a line. It falls. And so does the person who commits the same error attempting a headstand.

In Figure 4, the lines AB, AC, and BC represent about eighteen inches each, and the angles A, B, and C are all 60 degrees.

When you kick the feet up be sure you kick hard enough, and push well on the arms. The arms must bear a good portion of the weight, in spite of the fact that the head bears most. Especially on entering the stand do the arms bear weight. Do not push too much on them, however, or you will fall over backward. Be careful to push equally on both arms in maintaining balance. The biggest portion of the body weight rests on the top of the head. Be sure that you stand on the top of your head, rather than on the forehead or the back of your head.   The body should be straight, legs stiff, heels together, and toes pointed.

Variation: Headstand with back arched as in handstand.   This looks better but is more difficult to hold.

CARTWHEEL

In this stunt the limbs are outstretched and the whole body rigid so that it may roll in a vertical plane across the mats like a cartwheel (see diagram).   The hub of the wheel is at the navel, and the arms and legs, extended and separated, represent the spokes.   The rim of the wheel is altogether imaginary, but you must keep it in mind to have a perfect cartwheel.   Remember that the shape a rim takes depends on the spokes, and that a warped wheel has difficulty rolling.

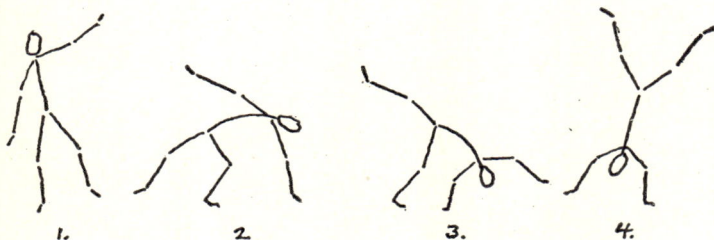

Stand erect and sidewise, with the feet about eighteen inches apart, toes pointed out.   The left foot should be pointed almost in the direction you will travel.   As a wind-up, a motion to help you get started, lean to the right putting all your weight on the right foot, lifting the left arm high, and left leg slightly, twisting the trunk

a little, and turning the head completely to the left
(Fig. 1).   To make the throw, swing down to the left,
bending left knee sharply and right slightly, placing the
left hand on the floor.   The right arm goes up as the
left goes down, and the right leg is lifted just before
the left hand touches (Fig. 2).   Following through,
the right arm goes over the head and the hand down
to the mat about two feet ahead of the left hand.   The
right leg is slung high over the body and the left leg
is lifted.   The body then goes to the inverted position
(Fig. 4), in which back and hips are straight, legs and
arms fully extended, well separated, and toes pointed.
The whole body is outstretched in a flat plane, which
leans neither to front nor back, but is vertical.   This
is the midpoint and the best looking position in the stunt.
Going beyond the midpoint, the positions are the same,
merely reversed, thus: Figures 1, 2, 3, 4, (and reversed)
3, 2, and 1.   You come out of a cartwheel just as you
go into it.   This whole throw must be done very
quickly, of course, and as a single motion, despite its
complication.

The tendency is for the beginner not to swing his
legs and feet high enough.   They must go directly
over the head in the inverted position.   The whole
body weight must be over the hands which are the base
and support.   Hold your head and neck straight; do
not duck as in the tuck.   Beginners often have difficulty
straightening the angles at hips, elbows, and knees.

There is also a tendency for them to twist their trunks, corkscrew fashion, in coming out of the flip.   Guard against these errors carefully.

In doing a series of cartwheels you will find it easy to go from one into another provided you keep your body straight and travel in a straight line.   The hands and feet must all touch on this line.   You must be well-balanced when you reach the upright position between each turn.   If you are not, stop, get your balance, and then proceed.   A series of cartwheels is not done well unless it is done rhythmically.   Pay careful attention to the time of each swing.   Roll smoothly and with rhythm.

Variations:

Roll first to left and then to right.

Knock your feet together when you reach the inverted position.

Turn when you regain upright position, and cartwheel again, thus going around in a circle.

Cartwheel with a jump (to be described later).

Snap-up or Kip

Stand as for forward roll, with feet and hands all eighteen inches apart (Fig. 1).   Duck your head under a little farther than for the simple roll, so that the back of your head touches about four inches behind a line drawn between the hands.   The hands will be doubled under very close to the shoulders when the shoulders roll onto the mat (Fig. 2).

4

Now comes the most important part, the snap.
There is a trick to it. You must not roll into the tuck
position, as is the natural tendency. You must bend
sharply in back and hips but leave your legs behind

1.   2.   3.   4.

you, knees only slightly bent and toes on the floor, until
the back of your neck touches (Fig. 2). Then is the
moment to throw. By holding back on the legs until
this point is reached, you get a wind-up, an opportunity for a long throw. This must be done with
force. The back muscles pull sharply, and at the same
time the whole body is raised by straightening the
arms, pushing up (Fig. 3). This springing out, and
pushing up with the arms, throws the body into the
air. The flip of the legs is carried on beyond the straight
line; belly is thrust up, back arched, and feet at finish
are doubled under to catch the weight of the body (Fig.
4.) Only by arching the back greatly and getting the
feet placed well under can the standing position be
gained easily. You will find it helpful at first to alight
with your feet about eighteen inches apart and toes
pointing outward. In this way you can get your feet
farther under you, and stand more easily.

Holding back on the legs at the start, and pushing with the arms in the middle of the roll is very important —and difficult. Practice them separately. The push with the arms must raise the whole body off the mat. Hands should be placed straight forward at the start. They will be bent back during the roll and throw. Arms lag behind as the body goes into the air and onto the feet (Fig. 4).

Once you master the trick you can come out of it in perfect reverse swan-dive position, and alight with very little impact.

It is sometimes hard to discover the right moment to throw. If you throw too soon, your shoulders will slide backwards on the mat. If you throw too late, you will not go high enough into the air to regain your feet. You must throw at just the moment when the back of the neck touches, and you must get your body weight over enough to flip forward rather than "back-fire."

Variations:

Do several snap-ups in series.

Begin from position flat on your back.

Turn the hands over, so that they face down, thumbs pointing out.

Snap-up from lying down position, placing hands on thighs, just above knees, and pushing with arms. This increases the force from the leg flip enough to serve as substitute for the push from the mat.

Snap-up without using your arms.

Snap-up from top of head instead of from shoulders. This stunt is called the headspring, and is often done with a run.

WALKING ON HANDS

Hand walking is easier than hand standing, just as on stilts it is easier to walk than to stand. All you need to do is get your body in the proper position, hold rigid, and maintain balance by stepping (with arms) in any direction your body leans and your weight tends

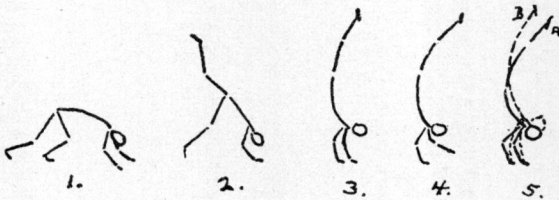

to overbalance. This is exactly the same principle one must learn in using stilts.

Stand with one foot ahead of the other. Stoop and place your hands (straight forward, fingers spread) on a line twelve inches ahead of the forward foot, and shoulder width apart (Fig. 1). Kick the feet up sharply, back foot first, the other immediately following (Fig. 2). Do not be afraid to kick over too far and do not walk away before the weight of your body is over your hands. Figure 3 represents the proper inverted position—back arched, legs together and perfectly rigid from hips to toes. "Locking" the legs, that is, tightening the muscles from hips to toes, is important for the same reason that it is easier to balance a rigid stick in your hand than a limber switch. Head is held up and toes are pointed.

As your body weight overbalances forward take a step in that direction to maintain the balance (Fig. 4). If it still overbalances forward take another step, and so on. If it overbalances to the side or backwards, take steps in those directions. You will learn with practice to overbalance in any direction you choose and thus walk wherever you like. The most common mistakes are, walking *out from under* the body weight, rather than walking *under* it; giving way in the arms and thus crumpling; waving the legs, and twisting at the waist. Be careful not to commit these errors.

You may be weak in the arms at first and not able to support your weight. Practice up against a wall. Place the hands about eighteen inches out from the wall and kick up to handstand position, touching the feet to the wall. Frequent repetition of this will strengthen your arms to bear the weight. You may even exercise them further by pushing up and down in this inverted position. Handstanding builds up the muscles in your arms and shoulders wonderfully. It is a quick strengthener.

Handstand

When you have learned to walk on your hands you have developed pretty well the sense of balance and have learned to control your body in the inverted position. The handstand calls for a fine sense of balance, excellent control, and a good deal of strength.

Take position as in Figure 1 on page 52, pushing the shoulders well forward, and stretching the hips well out behind. Put most of the weight on the fingers (which are widespread) rather than on the heel of the hand. Throw to the inverted position with one carefully executed kick. Do not move the hands. If you are not careful, you will walk away on all your trials and never learn to stand. Make it a rule not to walk at all in learning the stand. Figure 5 shows two positions, a low one (A) drawn with solid line, and a high one (B) with dotted line. By shifting from one of these positions toward the other you maintain balance after it is once gained. Drop to the lower position (A) when falling back (toward starting point) by bending the arms slightly, pushing the head and shoulders forward and bringing the feet forward with them. This tends to put more weight on the other side of the vertical over the base and correct the unbalanced condition. If the difficulty is in the other direction, raise up on the arms, lifting the head as high as you can, and throwing the feet back toward the

starting side, position (B).   This corrects the tendency
to fall over onto your back.   It may be helpful in
getting the balance to flex the knees a little.
But do not let them dangle. Once you gain
equilibrium, "lock" the legs.

Front Handspring

The handspring is the most difficult of the elementary
tumbling feats.   It calls for speed, strength, rhythm,
spring, and for real coordination.   Anyone who does
handsprings must be able to work the various
parts of his body smoothly together, to coordinate.
Coordination is the keynote of good tumbling, and this
should be a most important and valuable lesson for
every beginner.

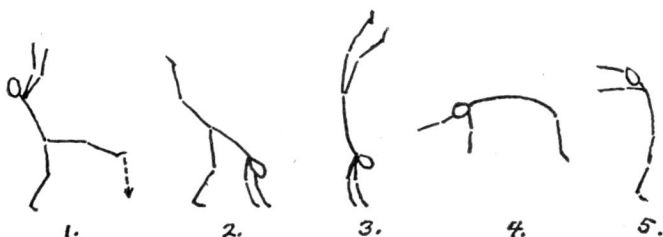

If you have not done the handspring before, better
use two thicknesses of mats.   Don't expect to conquer
all at once.   It takes time.   If you learn to handspring
quickly you should be greatly encouraged; but, if you
do not learn it quickly there is no need to be discouraged.
Follow directions carefully.

Prepare a run-way of at least ten paces. Run with moderate speed at first. You may quicken your run as you become more proficient. When you reach the mats and are ready to throw, lift the forward foot (preferably the left) and lean back slightly—at least do not lean forward—until the throw. Your arms are up and head tilted slightly back. This is the wind-up for the throw (Fig. 1).

There is a moment consumed in the wind-up during which time the momentum of your run tends to carry you forward. A balk seems necessary, but it is not. Avoid the balk by taking a little hop with the back foot. If this is too difficult for you to get at first, omit it and balk. When you are not running fast, the skip or hop is of small importance; but for the finished performance it must be employed. The rhythm of your run is lost otherwise, and the smoothness and grace of your stunt diminished.

From the wind-up position go into the throw (Figs. 2 and 3). The raised forward foot (left) is brought down sharply, about two feet ahead of the other as indicated in Figure 1. At the same time the body is bent forward and down toward the mat, arms extended ahead to receive the weight next. The hands are placed on a line about fifteen inches ahead of the forward foot. Immediately on being relieved of the body weight the back (right) foot flies into the air at the same moment that the trunk is bent forward

Planché three-high.

(Fig. 2). Thus a nearly straight line of back (right) leg, torso, and arms is preserved throughout (Figs. 1, 2, 3). The back foot must be lifted with force. Could you grasp a stone in your toes you should be able to throw it some distance with this motion. Also the upper part of the body should be brought down with force (Fig. 2). The handspring is not a dive or a leap, but a flip or spin. Imagine the navel as a pivot in Figure 2, and you can readily see how the body is spun or flipped when the fore part is thrown down with force and the legs thrown up. There is no leaping. The hands are placed on the mats, before the last foot leaves, and you jump with the feet only enough to throw them over your head, not to lift your body clear of the mats.

The arms should be held straight, stiff, and stretched out to as full a length as possible. You must keep your shoulders as far off the mats as you can. You may even resort to getting up on your fingertips for extra height. Actually your arms bend a little bit and considerable spring comes from them, but bending the arms too much is so bad a fault that we always caution beginners to keep the arms stiff.

As soon as the hands receive the weight of the body the back foot is thrown and brought up to the other (Fig. 3). The back is straightened, and then arched, as the bounce from the arms throws the body clear of the mats. A lay-out or reverse swan-dive position is taken for the finish of the stunt (Fig. 4). When you have done it perfectly you should come out of the handspring standing full height, head back, arms dragging after as in Figure 5.

While you are learning you may come out of it with legs bent, perhaps one lagging behind the other; you may be half-tucked, or have several other faults, but if you get onto your feet and make a stand, you have won most of the battle. Practice makes perfect.

Be careful not to run down at the mats. That is, do not double over forward on entering the stunt, not until the throw. The body should be erect as in Figure 1, just before the throw. In making the throw do not round the back too much or duck the head. The back should be almost straight and the arms in line with it. Much of an angle at the shoulders between the line of the arms and that of the torso hinders the handspring greatly. Head should be held up (Figs. 2 and 3). Most persons do not throw the feet hard enough. Flip your legs with all the strength you can muster.

There is usually a rough period of training to learning the handspring. You may save a lot of wear and tear on your body by always catching the shock of the fall on your feet instead of on your buttocks. Your feet should always lead the flip and be first to touch the mats in a fall. The hips are thrust up (forward) in taking the lay-out position, and the buttocks are raised so the feet may get under them. While you are learning it will be helpful to bend your knees alighting. When the main shock is dissipated by the feet, then the body may drop onto the mats without hurt.

Do not become discouraged. You may work along for months and not seem to be progressing, then all of a sudden the trick will break for you and be easy thereafter.

CHAPTER VI

ELEMENTARY TUMBLING—COMPANION

TUMBLING is most fun and most valuable when several people work together. Each can laugh at the other's difficulties. More important, each can criticize the other's form, and applaud his successes. Sociability tends to make all work play. It doubles the fun in tumbling.

You can do better work when you choose a partner, or two, and stick with him or them. No two men work alike. Partners learn each others' peculiarities and accommodate themselves to these. If you have worked some time with a partner you know what you can expect from him, and you behave accordingly. Confidence, not only in yourself, but in your partner is essential to accomplishment in this sport.

Usually a large and a small fellow work together, but it is just as well for partners to be the same size. Of course, large and small partners can do some stunts that twin partners cannot do; but the converse is also true. A team of two men of equal size always looks better, and the spectacular work can be more evenly divided. Having each man do an equal share, lends symmetry and balance to a performance.

For convenience we shall call one man always "Bottom," and the other "Topman," even though the names may not be indicative of their positions in any specific instance. The author selected these names for generally they suggest the part each man is to play. Because positions are sometime reversed during the course of a stunt, we avoided using the more frequently applied designations, "Topmounter" and "Understander," which definitely indicate position at a specific instance. It was felt that proper names of this kind would be less confusing and more satisfactory than such designations as A and B, No. 1 and No. 2.

FORWARD DOUBLE ROLL

Bottom lies on his back with his feet in the direction of travel. Topman stands at Bottom's shoulders,

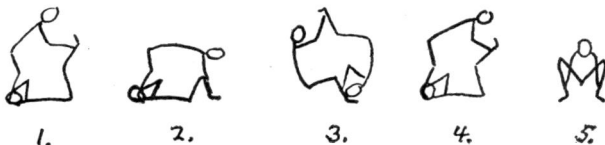

1.   2.   3.   4.   5.

feet along side of his ears, and facing in the direction of travel. Each grasps the other's ankles, hands straight in the easiest position, thumbs on one side, fingers on the other, just as one would grasp the steering wheel of an automobile. This is the most used grip in gymnastics, the *straight grip* (Fig. 1).

Topman leans forward placing Bottom's feet on the mat as close in to his buttocks as possible. Bottom of course must have his legs flexible. He knows where Topman will place them and aids. Bottom's knees are wide apart and feet closer together, so that Topman's arms may be held straight inside the knees (Fig. 5). Topman must not dive until Bottom's feet are placed upon the mat as in Figure 2. When this is done he has stability and can make his dive without wobbling. In diving let him be careful to duck his head in between Bottom's feet and as close to his buttocks as possible (Fig. 3). This avoids stretching "the roller" out so far that it would be uncontrollable. Bottom helps Topman go over by lifting Topman's feet a bit at the right moment. As the momentum of Topman's roll pulls his feet over, Bottom, holding on, comes up to sitting position and then to a crouched stand (Figs. 3 and 4).

Bottom then leans forward, places Topman's feet, dives and rolls. Topman comes up to his original position. One complete turn has been made. Three or four complete turns are usually made in series. Let the man on top remember to place the underman's feet before diving, to come in close as he dives and rolls, and to tuck his heels in close to his buttocks as he becomes the underman. Let the underman remember to keep his legs flexible, except for guiding while the feet are being placed; to separate his knees but bring his feet closer together; to aid the man on top in his motions as much as he can; and to come up at exactly the right moment.

It is a good stunt, and one any pair can do if they follow directions.

BACKWARD DOUBLE ROLL

This is the same as the forward double roll except in direction. It is a little more difficult to go backwards, but easy nevertheless.

Start from position of Figure 4. Topman sits or falls back with force, lifting his partner by the ankles as he goes down. Bottom pushes up with his arms as he rolls off the back of his neck, as in the simple backward roll (Fig. 3). Topman must hold up a bit with his arms as he becomes the under man, in order to support Bottom as he is carried over. Also, Topman lifts with his legs the moment Bottom's feet touch to aid the latter in gaining a stand (Figs. 2 and 1). Bottom then goes down and Topman comes over to complete a turn.

Let the man on top remember to sit close to his heels —with force—and to lift with his arms as he sits. As he becomes the under man he must with arms and legs hold his partner high above him. Let the under man remember to push with arms as he rolls up backwards, and to place his feet close to the shoulders of his partner as he regains a stand.

5

If you fall over to the side on either of these stunts,
it is because someone has failed to pull, push, or support
equally with both arms or legs.

Elephant Walk

Two men stand facing each other. Topman places
his hands on Bottom's shoulder. The latter grasps the
former at the sides (Fig. 1). Topman jumps, and at
the same time Bottom lifts him to a position straddling
the latter's chest as high up under the arms as possible
(Fig. 2). Topman locks his legs, by crossing his ankles
behind his partner. Then he lets himself swing back
till his hands touch the mat (Fig. 3). He works his

way between the legs of Bottom who may help by taking
a step forward. When Topman's shoulders are
through, Bottom falls forward onto his arms. Topman
places his hands on Bottom's heels and straightens his
arms which action pushes his chest and head high
(Fig. 3). In this position Bottom walks forward on all
fours, Topman swinging rhythmically with the
motion.

When the pair have walked far enough, Bottom may stoop, by bending elbows and knees, and Topman can drop easily to the mat on his belly (Fig. 4).

A more difficult but much better way to finish the stunt is for Bottom to straighten up to standing position, dragging Topman back through his legs (Fig. 5), to place his hands under Topman's back and both lift to the position of Figure 2, from which Topman can be let easily down onto his feet.   The difficulty of this finish varies inversely as the difference in size of the partners.

The Camel Walk

In the camel walk Topman lies down on his belly, feet extended, legs slightly separated, arms drawn in.

1.   *2.*   *3.*   *4.*

His partner stands at his heels facing him (Fig. 1). Bottom steps between Topman's legs, catches him around the thighs, and lifts him up wheelbarrow fashion (Fig. 2). Topman locks his own legs around his partner and works his way through his partner's legs as in the elephant walk, except that he is facing opposite and bends his spine forward instead of backward (Fig. 3).   Bottom bends forward for walking on all fours.

Topman places his hands on Bottom's heels and straightens his arms, lifting his head and shoulders high. Bottom walks forward (Fig. 4).

Topman must not clasp his partner too closely with his legs. He should hang almost loosely to allow the free swinging motion that adds so much to the appearance of this stunt.

The stunt is finished as the elephant walk; except, on difficult finish, when Bottom straightens up, he should carry Topman only so far as position in Fig. 2, then give him a shove forward into a simple roll.

Back To Back And Over (Wringer)

Two men stand back to back, with their arms up (Fig. 1). Either one of them grasps the other's wrists with the straight grip. Since there is little strain here, one holds for both. Topman, who is going over, places his shoulders just a bit above and on the shoulders of Bottom.

1.   2.   3.   4.   5.

Bottom begins the motion by pulling on the arms and leaning forward. Topman picks up his feet, and without sliding down at all, curls up and rolls over the back of Bottom (Fig. 2). His body is balanced and held right by the arms. In rolling off the back of Bottom, Topman's feet must be leading his motion. They must be well ahead of the rest of his body (Fig. 3). If they are not, Topman will not stand when he hits the mat, but will crumple or alight on his knees. Figure 4 shows position at the end of the stunt.

It is usual to do several wringers in succession. The same man may go over again or the partner may take turns rolling. From position in Figure 4, without loosening the grip, let them tip up the circle of their arms and get underneath it (Fig. 5), thus turning back to back again and assuming the original starting position (Fig. 1). If the same man goes over each time the pair will remain in about the same spot with no progression. If a different one goes over each time there will be a forward progression in the direction Bottom faces.

Let Topman not pick up his feet until he feels Bottom lifting him. Then let him curl up to half-tuck position. He must not arch. He must roll straight steadying himself with the arms. Both men must pull equally on both arms. Let Bottom take care not to lose his balance. He must place his feet well apart and hold all the weight over the base they afford. Be sure that the feet of the man on top lead the motion of the roll and come down to the mat first. Don't loosen the grip between turns.

Shoulder Balance

Bottom lies on his back, knees flexed and up, heels close in to buttocks and about hip-width apart. The toes are pointed out so that, viewed from above, thighs, forelegs, and feet are in a line. This position of the legs makes the strongest support. Topman stands at Bottom's toes, facing him (Fig. 1).

1.   *2.*   *3.*   *4.*

Topman places his hands, straight grip from top, on his partner's knees, and leans forward placing his shoulders in Bottom's hands (Fig. 2). Bottom's hands are held straight, thumbs along side of fingers, cup-shaped, and are placed on the tips of his partner's shoulders. Topman then, pushing with arms as in headstand, kicks up to an inverted balance (Figs. 3 and 4). His shoulders, the main points of support, should be over Bottom's chest and not over his abdomen. Bottom's arms should be straight.

Let Topman remember that he has four points to his base, the tips of his two shoulders and his two hands. Pressure must not be taken from any of these. Gripping the knees with the hands so that one may pull on them as well as push is often an aid to attaining balance.

There are several other balances the pair may do.

BELLY BALANCE:

[See illustration p. 72]

Bottom is on his back as before, but with hips and knees flexed, feet raised. Topman places Bottom's feet, straight and together, on his abdomen and grips hands with Bottom. He then leans forward, putting his weight on Bottom's feet and pulls with the arms. Bottom straightens his knees, raising Topman to the final position which is an arch (Fig. 1).

SITTING BALANCE:

[See illustration p. 72]

Bottom is down as before, but with arms on the mats a little away from his side. Topman stands backwards with his heels at Bottom's buttocks. He places Bottom's feet, straight and together, on his seat and holds them with his hands, until his weight is shifted altogether to them, and he is raised by Bottom to the final position. Then he extends his arms to the sides (Fig. 2).

STANDING BALANCE:

This is more difficult and should be considered advanced work. But logically it belongs with the other three balances. It requires a good deal of practice.

Bottom is on his back again with arms by his side. His thighs are doubled over on his abdomen as far as possible without raising his back from the mat. Forelegs are pointing straight up. Topman steps onto his partner's thighs steadying himself by holding on to the vertical forelegs. He shifts his weight slowly to the right foot, raising the other and placing it on top of Bottom's right foot (Fig. 3). Holding Bottom's feet

1.   2.   3.   4.

together with his hands, he slowly shifts the weight to this high (left) foot, and raises his own right to a place alongside of his own left foot and on top of Bottom's left foot. He is then in a squat position on top of Bottom's feet holding all four feet together with his hands. From this he rises slowly to the erect position (Fig. 4).

When you can do this stunt you have developed a very good sense of balance.

KNEE ROLL

Bottom is on his back, legs drawn in as for shoulder balance. Topman comes running with moderate speed, from the direction of the feet, places his hands on Bottom's knees, and begins the roll (Fig. 1). The roll is taken with a little dive, but the hands remain on the knees and support a good part of the weight (Fig. 2). The duck and turn must take place over Bottom's lower chest, not over his hips or abdomen. Bottom puts his hands on Topman's shoulder blades, as he comes rolling, and pushes upward and forward (Fig. 3).

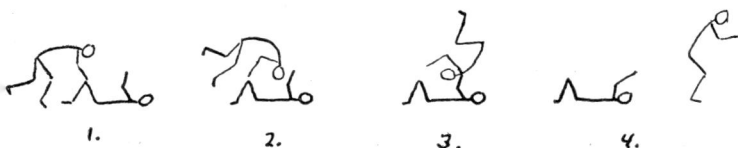

1. 2. 3. 4.

This serves to hold Topman's body a little more than knee-high during the roll, and to carry him over onto his feet on the mat beyond (Fig. 4). Topman must not handspring, but roll. His back must be rounded not arched, and his whole body in the half-tuck position as he goes over. He must be careful to keep up at least knee-high, and to turn far enough forward to meet Bottom's hands over his chest.

Topman must be careful not to duck his head between Bottom's knees and turn over his hips. He must not forget to roll, and do his own turning. Bottom only supports him. He should come out of the stunt in half-tuck position, not fully erect (Fig. 4).

ANKLE PICK-UP

Pick-ups are tricky ways for one fellow to toss another onto his feet from lying or sitting positions on the mat.

In the ankle pick-up, Topman is lying on his back, feet raised, and hands on the mat behind his shoulders as in the snap-up. Bottom stands facing him at his buttocks (Fig. 1).

Bottom grasps Topman's ankles (straight forward grip). In getting ready to throw, he bends over, pushing Topman's relaxed legs down for a wind-up (Fig. 2). Then comes the throw. Bottom jerks up sharply with all his force, straightening his legs and pushing out

1. 2. 3. 4.

against Topman's heels as he lifts. Topman at the same time springs up, flexing his legs against his partner's outward lift and pushing against the floor with his arms (Fig. 3). The combination of these forces throws him into the air, in half-tuck position, turning in the direction of his feet (Fig. 4). He comes out of this very nicely onto his feet and regains the upright position, facing his partner.

Teeter-totter.

Bottom must lift hard and push out with force. Topman tightens his legs against his partner's moves, and pushes up hard with his arms. He had better keep his eyes open and watch for the floor while spinning.

TEETER-TOTTER OR SEE-SAW

The two men face each other, gripping arms. Topman jumps up to straddle Bottom's waist (Fig. 1). Straightening and stiffening his legs, and holding on with the arms, Topman slides down, until Bottom's knees press in the middle of the under side of his thigh,

1.   2.   3.   4.

and his own feet, turned pigeontoed, are held against the shoulder blades of Bottom. The arms of both partners approximate the position of hands folded in the lap. Bottom's arms in this position can be clamped down on Topman's legs to help hold them in place (Figs. 2 and 3). When this position is attained, Bottom rocks the whole arrangement by flexing and unflexing his knees: first position of Figure 2, then position of Figure 3; position 2 again, and position 3—"see-saw, Marjorie Daw."

When it is desired to finish the stunt, Bottom can rock down hard, falling onto his back, and placing Topman's feet on the floor. The momentum of the fall is sufficient to bring Topman to a stand, whence he dives over his partner's head onto the mat beyond all in one motion (Fig. 4).

Bottom has a very difficult task balancing the arrangement on the rather small base of his own two feet, especially when rocking. He must be very careful of his balance. Topman must see that he is poised properly on the tips of his partner's knees with his own toes locked securely behind the latter's shoulder blades under his arms. He must keep his knees straight, which is no easy job, and he must round his back enough to make it point generally in a direction parallel to Bottom's.

During the rocking the partners may twiddle their thumbs. This adds a comedy touch.

STEP-MOUNT

Bottom stands staunchly with feet apart and pointing out, knees and hips bent slightly, back straight and perpendicular. Topman stands very close at his left side, facing him. The partners turn toward each other as much as possible without moving the feet, and grasp hands. The left hands may be grasped straight forward, as for shaking, but right hands must be twisted over so that no change will be required in reaching final

position.   Each partner turns his right palm up toward
the other's face, thumbs down, and grasp.   Topman
lifts his left foot and places it on Bottom's left thigh
close to his crotch (Fig. 1).

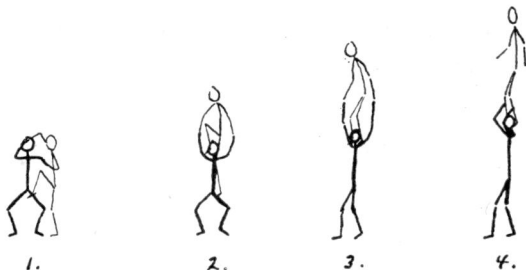

1.   2.   3.   4.

In mounting, Topman rises up on his left leg, throwing
the right arms over Bottom's head, and places his
right foot on the latter's right shoulder (Fig. 2).   Bottom aids with the arms.   Topman then puts his weight
onto his right leg and lifts his left foot to his partner's
left shoulder.   There he stands in a half-crouched position, steadying himself with the arms.

As Topman's body weight is transferred (Fig. 3) to
the shoulders from the thigh, Bottom straightens up
full height.   He has a heavy weight on his shoulders
and a hard job to balance.   He must be careful not to
pull Topman too far forward with the arms.   He must
stand erect, head up, chest out, and arms straight
above.

In taking the final position they break the hand grip,
Topman points his toes and places his shins against

the back of Bottom's head which is pressed back for
the purpose; Bottom clasps his hands on top and
behind his partner's calves, and pulls forward and down.
Thus we have a good solid junction of the two figures.
Topman straightens up except for a slight bend in his
knees (Fig. 4).

In mounting, the partners must be careful to keep all
their weight over the small base, Bottom's two feet.
Bottom must not lean forward too much or pull forward with his arms.   The usual tendencies are for Topman to swing out too far in mounting, thus upsetting
the balance and for Bottom to pull his partner over
forward with the arms, after the latter's feet are in
place on the shoulders.   Avoid these tendencies.

Once in final position the pair may walk or run in any
direction and make quick turns without losing their
balance.   Falling forward without a break until the

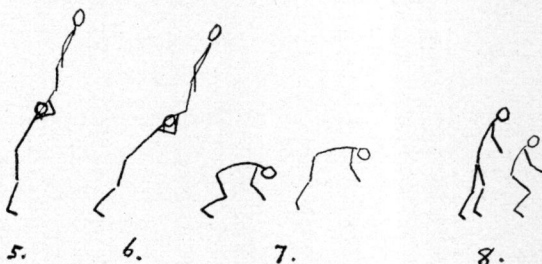

5.   6.   7.   8.

last moment is a favorite stunt.   The pair stands erect,
and gradually overbalances forward (Fig. 5).   They
hold together until they are about half way down and

look as though they would crash on their faces (Fig. 6).
Then they break, each going onto his feet, overbalanced
forward (Fig. 7), and into a simple roll.

The usual way of coming down from the two high
positions is to overbalance forward (Fig. 5), and Topman drops easily onto his feet (Fig. 8).   This is much
better than having Topman jump, as jumping is rough
on Bottom's shoulders and neck.

Straddle, Front and Back

In doing the front straddle, two partners stand facing
each other.   Topman stoops over placing his shoulder
tips on his knees and his arms between his legs, fists
together.   Bottom leans over him straddling his neck,
and grasps his wrists with a straight grip (Fig. 1).

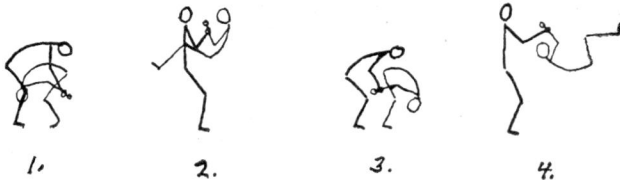

In the throw Bottom begins the motion by pulling
up sharply with the arms.   Topman helps at the take-
off by jumping from his toes.   He is lifted into the
air and turns a roll straddling the arms which are his
sole support (Fig. 2).   He comes easily out of this onto
his feet again facing Bottom, who does not release the
hand grip until they are both standing again facing
each other.

6

Bottom must lift his partner high, so that the turn will take place at shoulder height, and on his forearms. Topman must hold his tuck until the turn is done and he is ready to drop his feet to the mat again.

In the back straddle the two stand facing in the same direction. Topman stoops over as before and his partner grasps his wrists (Fig. 3). Bottom is in very much the same position as for the ankle pick-up. On the throw he jerks up sharply and lifts as high as possible, pushing forward at the same time. Bottom releases his grip as soon as he has lifted and pushed. Topman spins onto his feet in half-tuck position.

In both stunts Bottom grips Topman's wrists so that his thumbs are on top, straight forward grip. In front straddle Bottom does not release the grip until the stunt is done. In the back straddle, he releases with the throw.

In both stunts Topman must be very careful to keep his legs wide-spread so they will not strike Bottom's body but straddle it.

Planché

The two men stand facing in the same direction. Bottom behind, places his hands on Topman's waist, the latter grasping with his own hands Bottom's wrists (Fig. 1). Topman gives a little jump and Bottom lifts him to the position of Figure 2, standing on the latter's thighs. Bottom then shifts his hands, one at a time,

to his partner's knees, then leans back, and allows his
partner to lean forward a little.   Topman arches his
back and bends his knees slightly; his arms are extended
to the sides (Fig. 3).

1.   2.   3.   4.

To have a perfect planché the two partners must get
just the right lines with their forms.   The lines of their
torsos should be pretty nearly parallel.   Topman must
not be too far forward, but should keep nearly over the
base.   Bottom's back must be straight, not rounded.

When you get into the position of Figure 2, open out
slowly so that you will not overbalance.

Figure 4 shows a nearly similar pose in which the
wrists are locked Indian grip, and the line of the two
figures allowed to diverge more.   Both poses are used
frequently in pyramids.

CHAPTER VII

ADVANCED TUMBLING—INDIVIDUAL

THE titles of this and the two chapters preceding may be a little misleading. There is no sharp line between elementary and advanced tumbling, no more than there is a sharp line between day and night. One blends into the other. Your progress from the stunts of the last chapter to the stunts of this one will be as easy as turning the pages between. Only understand that you are doing advanced work now. Be more careful and more patient. You are supposed to have mastered fundamentals, so instructions will be less explicit than heretofore.

EGG ROLL

Stand erect and backwards, at the edge of the mat. Sit down with force as for backward roll, catching the shock on your arms, and roll up to the back of your neck (Fig. 1). The egg-roll is the same as the simple backward roll up to the midpoint where the body is over the head, except that it is more forceful. At the midpoint the body is straightened from the half-tuck position, and arched to form a "rocker" on which to

roll down (Fig. 2). The straightening must be well
timed, quickly and carefully done so as not to upset
the roll. The arms bear most of the weight, to keep
the face from rubbing the mat. Holding the arch
rigid, rock down, first onto the chest, then abdomen,
etc. (Fig. 3). If you hold the arch rigid you will rock
easily onto your knees. By pushing up with the arms
at the moment when the lower half of your body slaps
the mats you lift the upper half clear of the mat (Fig.
4). With a little jump from the knees, at the same
time you push with the arms, you may get your legs
under you, and come up to a standing position (Fig.
5). This last should be done slowly continuing the
rhythm of the roll. The knees are straightened slowly
and the arms are lifted as you rise.

It is a very pretty trick when done smoothly from
stand to stand.

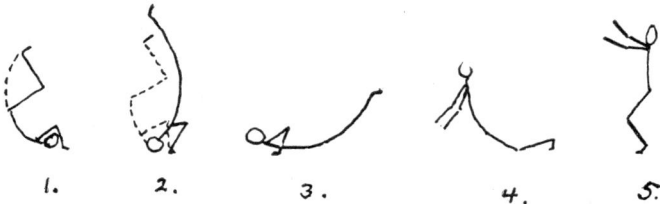

l.   2.   3 .   4.   5.

You must sit down with force, and when you reach
the inverted position, straighten out with force. Get
your timing right; otherwise you will bump your seat,
or the back of your head. As you roll over remember
to straighten your arms slightly so as to lift most of the

weight from your face. In rocking down hold the arch rigid. If you loosen up or flex the hips in the slightest degree, you will hit flat. When you rock down, the shock is shifted from chest to abdomen, to hips, thighs, knees, and onto your toes. The force of the fall is thus conserved and can be used to help bring you back up to a stand.

You may practice the rocker by standing on your hands, and dropping onto your chest for the rock, or slap, as it is usually called. Or simply stand on your knees, assume the arch, and rock forward. This last rocker is, of course, reversed but involves the same principle.

FALL FORWARD TO HANDSTAND

This is another rocker stunt. Stand facing the mat, with slightly bent knees and arched back (Fig. 1). Overbalance forward, falling first onto the knees (Fig.

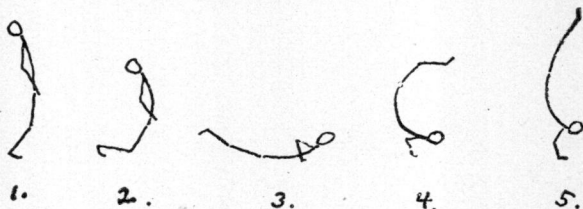

1. 2. 3. 4. 5.

2), then rocking down. The weight is shifted from the knees to the thighs and hips, to the abdomen, and to the chest and arms. You must reach for the mat with your arms as you fall, being careful all the while not to break your arch. As your torso comes onto the mat

the arms are doubled alongside the chest and protect
the head and chin from striking the mat (Fig. 3).
As the weight rolls onto the forepart of the rocker the
latter part rises from the mat.   At this point accentuate
the arch in your back, bend the knees slightly, and push
up with your arms as hard as possible (Fig. 4).   This
lifts the whole body up toward the final handstand
position (Fig. 5).

It is not a difficult stunt provided you have a good
arch and strength in your arms.   Coordination of course
is essential.

High Kick and Slap

This is still another rocker.   The performer runs in,
kicks the right leg high into the air in front of him, and
at the same time jumps with the left leg.   This begin-

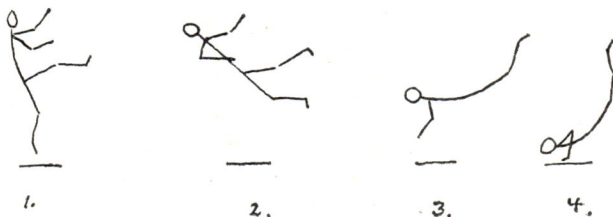

1.   2.   3.   4.

ning is a little like the punt in football, or even more like
tour jeté in dancing (Fig. 1).   As you reach the top of
the leap make a quick half twist to the left (as in tour
jeté), turning face downward (Fig. 2).   The head
should be thrown low and the feet up high since you

must assume approximately a dive position (Fig. 3) for landing. The arms catch the weight as in the dive, but instead of tucking and rolling you "slap" the mat, or rock down (Fig. 4), going onto your feet as in the egg roll.

This stunt requires good control in the air. Like the forward and backward rolls it is an excellent safety measure.

VERTICAL TURN

This stunt is used very often in the Russian dance.

Stand erect with feet about twelve inches apart and toes out. For a wind-up, bend the knees and twist the

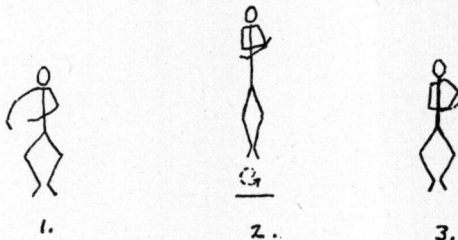

1.　　　　2.　　　　3.

torso to the right, arms out slightly accentuating the twist (Fig. 1). Begin the throw by swinging the arms sharply to the left, twisting the body in that direction and springing with the legs. The body must be perfectly straight, knees practically straight, and toes pointed as you spin in the air; the least bend of the back will throw you off balance. The motion on the throw particularly of the arms, is around and up, turning and lifting. You can use your feet to help give the spin at the take-off. Arms are bent slightly, and held out a little in front of the chest as you turn (Fig. 2). You come down as you went up, but take the shock of the fall on your toes, and by bending the knees, especially the latter. Ease off the spin by twisting to the left as you reach the floor (Fig. 3). To do one turn is easy; to do two is not. To do three turns is very difficult. Some experts do four and five. The trick lies particularly in the way you throw the arms, in jumping high, and in holding straight. Keep your eyes open, and if you can, turn the head to look always in one direction, except for an instant between each turn when you jerk it around.

BUCK

The performer stands straight, in the middle of the mat. Beginning the buck, he dives forward onto his arms as a bucking horse would dive onto his forelegs. The dive must be up and down, not merely down or out. The course he travels must be an arch (Fig. 1).

The arms take all the shock of the dive and hold the weight of the body for a moment in the crouched handstand position (Solid Fig. 1). Legs are drawn in, hip and knee joints both being flexed. These are not bent during the dive but after the landing. Their flexibility, with that of the elbows, eases the shock of landing.

From this crouched inverted position the performer
springs, by kicking hard out in the air and pushing on
his arms at the same moment with all his strength.
This throws his body into the air, back toward the

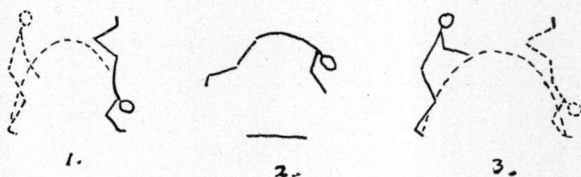

1.   2.   3.

original position (Fig. 2). The course of travel back
is arched, like the dive forward, but a little lower. The
performer alights on his feet and is prepared for the
second buck forward (Fig. 3), which comes immediately. A series of four or five bucks makes an interesting stunt.

The most difficult part is throwing from the hands
hard enough to regain the upright position. The trick
of it lies in a vigorous kick out into the air, and a good
hard push at exactly the same moment. Don't forget
to flex the knees, hips, and elbows as you dive to the
handstand. When you do a series, pay attention to
rhythm.

CARTWHEELS WITH JUMPS

In an earlier chapter we described cartwheels in
detail. The jumps are merely inserted between
turns.

Throw a cartwheel, and as you come onto your feet jump straight up into the air, turning all the while, and bending sidewise at the waist in the direction of

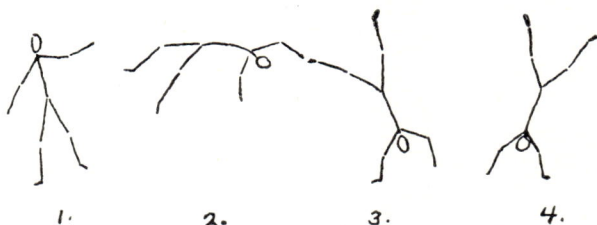

1.   *2.*   *3.*   *4.*

the mat (Fig. 2). The leap must be high and the feet flipped over so that you can alight on your hands with your feet almost directly above (Fig. 3). The cartwheel follows naturally and easily (Fig. 4). As you come onto your feet, leap again with all your strength, using every bit of the momentum of the turn in your throw.

Remember to turn fast and to flip your legs as you jump. It takes a great deal of spring and throw to do this well. A series of three or four cartwheels with jumps is a beautiful display.

TAKE-OFF

The take-off is of course not a stunt in itself, but an important lead to stunts. You should know how to do well a running take-off from two feet. The run should be smooth and light. It should not be too long. Fifty feet is plenty in any case. The last step preliminary to jumping, which is called the "pounce," should be just a little longer and considerably higher than the others. The dotted line in Figures 1 and 2 show the mean course through which your feet travel. Note that the pounce is high and short, not low and long as many beginners do it. If the pounce is high and short the dive tends likewise to be high and short.

The two are alike except that the curve of the dive is on a much larger scale. You will find it decidedly advantageous to leap high and short rather than low and long.

At the jump the arms should be above the shoulders as in Figure 3. This is the best position of the arms in taking-off for all tumbling dives and the front somersault. Notice that on the pounce the arms are bent at the same time the legs are bent, and on the throw

1.   2.   3.   4.

they are extended the same time the legs are extended. For the dive handspring and the somersault the arms must go up on the take-off (Fig. 4) so they can be thrown down to aid in turning. If you find difficulty getting them up for these two stunts try running in with arms up from the start, until you get used to having them in that position.

Keep the body leaning forward at the take-off. Never lean backward, or even have your body straight vertical, on the take-off. Doing so will kill the advantage of your run. You should be leaning slightly forward; and keep moving in that direction. This take-off is quite different from the springboard take-off used in water-diving. You may have trouble learning it, but don't give up; it is well worth the effort.

The Dive Handspring

This stunt is quite similar in principle to the cartwheel with a jump. It is a running dive with handspring finish.

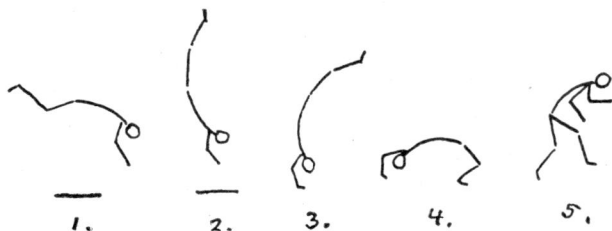

The performer gets a good run, takes-off from both feet as just described, throwing the legs high and shoulders low (Fig. 1). As the feet rise into the air, assume the lay-out position (Fig. 2). Hands are first to touch, and arms receive about half the shock. The feet, having been flipped over, carry the body weight ahead of the support of the arms (Fig. 3), causing it to fall toward the mat beyond the point where the hands touch. The body being arched as for the handspring the weight falls on the feet which are tucked under to catch the balance of the shock (Fig. 4). As the feet hit, push with the arms and flip the upper half of your body. This throws you onto your feet, and you can continue running (Fig. 5).

The stunt is easy to do roughly, but difficult to do well. The arms must be above the shoulders during the pounce and leap. Flip your legs hard and high at the take-off. Excellent leg work is required.

Front Somersault

The front somersault is the first of the difficult air-turns we shall tackle. The performer must leap into the air and make a complete turn, end over end, coming down on his feet standing upright or continuing the run.

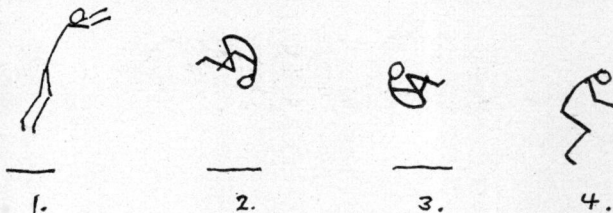

1.   2.   3.   4.

Run about twenty paces and take-off from two feet as described above (Fig. 1). When you reach the top of the leap, tuck! The movement is quite complicated. Throw the head forward and down, rounding

Belly pitch.

the shoulders sharply; bring in the legs till the knees and chest touch; throw the arms down with force, grasping the shins just below the knees, elbows bent, thumbs and fingers together. The knees should be slightly separated and your chin between them. The arms should pull the legs in tight to the body thus making a compact ball (Fig. 2). This tucking motion is begun by a downward throw of arms, head, and shoulders. That throw should come at the top of the jump. It spins the ball and accounts for the somersault (Fig. 3). The tighter your tuck the faster you spin. When you have turned almost over, open your tuck and alight standing, in a half crouched position (Fig. 4). You may stop completely, continue running, or take a simple roll. Your choice of these three alternatives will depend largely on how far over you get. Often you will go over too far, and the roll should be taken as a protective measure to keep you from going flat on your face.

It is almost impossible for the beginner, or even for the good tumbler who hasn't tried the somersault before, to step right up and do one. It takes plenty of practice. And in practicing the beginner had better "start at the bottom and work up." This we mean literally.

At least three thicknesses of mats should be used for a starter. Run in easily and do a simple dive roll. Remember to catch the shock on your shoulders, not

7

on your head. Next trial do the same without using your arms. You must clear your head and light on your back. It is not necessary to jump more than a foot or so to do this and it will not hurt in the least. Practice until you can throw over easily onto your back, and tuck fairly well. The tuck is the most important part so master it well before you try much of a jump. The jumps, even when low, should be short. Do not waste your strength covering too much distance. As you become more proficient increase the height of your jump a little at a time. Do not increase it more than you can conveniently manage. You can judge your own success best, and you need go no faster or higher than you like. This stunt is thought to be very dangerous and tumblers are supposed to take a lot of "punishment" learning it. If you follow the directions given here, you can reduce the punishment to the minimum, and eliminate altogether the danger.

During the learning period, hold your tuck until after you have landed. Don't try to open out, until you are satisfied that you can get easily over onto your feet; then start increasing your jump and breaking your tuck to keep from going over too far. Do it cautiously, being sure to keep your eyes open to see when to break. A good spotter can help considerably by slapping you behind the neck and helping to spin you over faster.

The take-off is practically the same as for the high dive. Especially try to get up high in the air. Reach far up with the arms as you mount, and throw the arms down hard as you tuck.

On the pounce and the take-off be sure that your figure is tipped slightly forward, and that you keep moving in the direction of your run.

Don't be at all discouraged about the length of time it takes to learn the somersault. It is a difficult stunt, and when you have accomplished it you have really earned congratulations.

Back Somersault

The back somersault is much easier to do than the front somersault, but there is a trick to it. Fewer people do back somersaults simply because the technic is less widely known.

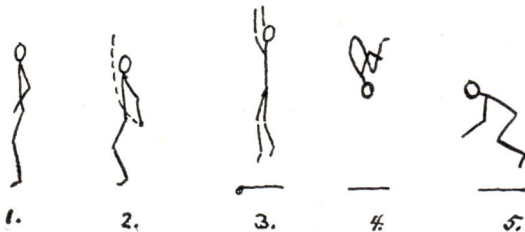

A belt will be found very helpful. It allows the beginner to work out details of his form without hurting himself. It gives confidence, and makes it possible for him to master the stunt much more quickly. Belts are famous for getting in the way, but the back somersault affords little opportunity for tangling in the ropes. This stunt is quite simple for anyone with good coordination and strength.

Stand on the mats, erect, head up (Fig. 1). The arms begin the movement. Swing them back and slightly out, dipping in the knees at the same time. The dip is your wind-up, and takes place in the half-second previous to jumping. When you have reached the position of Figure 2, swing the arms in across your chest and straight up (Dotted line Fig. 2). Put your whole body weight behind that arm movement, just as if you were delivering upper-cut blows with both fists, either of which would lift your body off the ground. The moment you swing with your arm, jump. In preparing for the jump bend the knees only moderately and take-off from the toes. A quick springy jump from the toes and slightly bent knees is much better than that which comes from a deep bend and a long pushing take-off which must necessarily be slower. Bend about as much as illustrated; and keep torso vertical, head up (Fig. 2). Both the jump and the arm throw are quick as a flash, and lift the body high into the air, straight up (Fig. 3). Note that in Figure 3 the arms are above the shoulders, the head is back, and the trunk is straight.

When you reach the height of your jump—tuck! The back tuck is a little different from the front. You do not throw the head and shoulder down, but bring the knees up to the chest, toss the head back forcibly, and pull harder with the arms on the knees, (Fig. 4). When you have learned to do this tuck right you will spin like a cannon ball.

As you throw your head back keep the eyes open and watch for the ground. When you see the ground and feel that you have turned almost completely over, break your tuck and come down standing. You should alight about two feet behind where you started (Fig. 5).

In learning this stunt practice the jump and the tuck separately. Get height with your jump, and just go straight up—not backwards or forward. Make the most of the lift you get from the swing of your arms. Practice bringing your knees up for the tuck without turning. You can do this by standing erect, jumping, bringing up your legs, clasping your knees, and letting them drop again as you come down without having turned over. This is the same as the tuck in the stunt except for the toss of the head and the throw over backward.

When you put jump and tuck together and try to somersault, have someone help you, either by holding the belt or by spotting. Remember that not the slightest interval may elapse between jump and tuck. You must work with exceeding rapidity to get over before you alight.

When you can get over onto your feet with help, try it alone. You should at least be able to get to your knees without help. If you can get that far you won't hurt yourself. So have no fear. Fear, more than anything else, will spoil your stunt. As we said before, however, this does not mean for you to be foolhardy; only bold.

BACK HANDSPRING OR FLIP-FLOP

A good series of back handsprings is one of the prettiest stunts a tumbler can do, and at the same time one of the hardest. Many people execute simple handsprings but few can do a smooth series of backs. Even with professionals it is necessary to practice consistently and often to keep back handsprings perfect.

Stand as for back somersault. Dip deeper, and fall backward as you begin to dip (Fig. 1). On the throw, swing the arms out in front and up; throw the head back, the abdomen and hips up (forward) making an arch of your back. At the same time jump with your

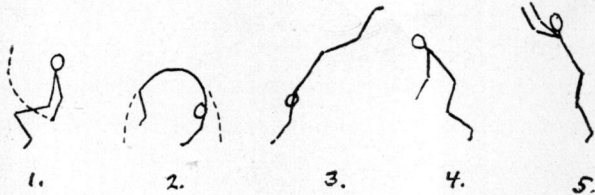

1.   2.   3.   4.   5.

legs enough to produce a little backward dive up and down. The back must be arched to this course of flight (Fig. 2). Arms must be directly below the head and shoulders as the hands touch the mat, and must bear most of the shock, as in a forward dive. The hands touch the mats about two feet behind the heels. When they touch flip the legs over by sharply flexing the hips and contracting the abdominal muscles (Fig. 3). When the legs pass the vertical, push hard with the arms and spring onto your feet, as in the buck. You will not need to kick out, however, for sufficient momentum to put you on your feet is derived from the flip. Pulling the legs down from the inverted position must be done snappily. Whip them down! They must strike the mat with a bang. Here is where most of your speed is derived. You alight in a half-crouched position leaning forward, but with momentum to keep on going (Fig. 4). A single handspring is usually finished by a jump into the air which dissipates this extra momentum and gives an impression of forcefulness and grace (Fig. 5). In doing a series of handsprings this jump is omitted. You go into the second flip from the position of Figure 4. With a backward moving impetus from the first flip, you fall easily into position for the second. There is no time interval between the two. One flows smoothly into the other. Four or five flip-flops are usually done to a series.

A back somersault on the end gives the stunt a beautiful finish and makes it startlingly impressive.

In learning the back handspring use the belt, or have a good spotter to help you. Practice the dip first, and get the idea of falling back as you dip. In learning the throw don't try to put too much force into it. The

throw is a flip, not a jump. Jump with your legs only
enough to throw the lower part of your body up and
over; and to get in the back dive position.

In good flip-flops the performer's center of mass actually does not rise on the throw but acts as a hub around
which the body spins. For the beginner, however, it is
better to accentuate the dive to allow more height and
the opportunity to get farther under yourself with arms
and shoulder. It is necessary to bend the back a great
deal and to place your hands close to your heels.
Otherwise you will not be able to flip the legs over (Fig.
2).

In beginning it is a good idea to practice dipping and
swinging the arms correctly. Hold them straight and
swing in front of you and up, looking always in the
direction they point (Dotted line, Fig. 1). When you
have carried them as far around as possible in the standing position, they are up and back, your head is tilted
back, your torso is arched (as in Fig. 2 from belt to
hands) and knees bent. Then you have reached the
point to throw. Jump up and slightly back, making a
dive over the course shown in dotted line Figure 2. If
you jump fairly high, take a good arch, and then pull the
legs down sharply, you will go over easily. Don't
forget to catch the shock on your arms and to keep
your arms straight as a protection for your head.

If you tend to fall forward and not progress easily in
the backward direction as you should, you are probably

neglecting to overbalance backward as you dip. Accentuate that motion.

Don't forget to bend the back sufficiently and to whip the legs over fast.

It is a difficult stunt, but a beautiful one, and well worth your practice.

CHAPTER VIII

ADVANCED TUMBLING—COMPANION

The work of this chapter will perhaps cause more all-round enjoyment than that of any other chapter. The stunts are moderately easy and yet spectacular enough to make a good show. They are companion work, so there is sociability added to the individual physical enjoyment. If you work carefully and try hard, you will be able to learn all these stunts and do them well.

High Roll

Bottom lies on his back, feet up, arms on the mats behind his shoulders. Topman stands in the palms of his hands, and grasps with his own hands Bottom's insteps from the top or sole side (Fig. 1). On the first count Topman presses hard with his arms on Bottom's feet, and at the same time jumps up toward position 2, wherein his back is horizontal and his limbs vertical, making right-angles at hip and shoulder joints. As Topman executes these motions Bottom counteracts them. He resists the pressure on his feet by holding his legs straight which must support a good part of

Topman's weight.   He acts against the jump with his arms enough to lift the balance of Topman's weight up to arm's length.   This is done with a jerk and is the greatest exertion in the stunt.   The underman's arms have the greatest strain (Fig. 2).   The performers are now in the best looking phase of the stunt, the "box" position.   Hold the pose a moment.   A touch of comedy may be added if the man on top will turn his head mechanically to face the audience as he comes up to this position each time, then straight again before he goes down.   It takes about two seconds to do this which is just the right length of time to hold the "box."

On the second count they come back to the original position (Fig. 1).   In lowering let Bottom bend his legs slightly as well as his arms, to keep Topman's back approximately horizontal.   Without changing grips, on the third count, Topman dives over as in the simple double roll.   Both men keep the muscles of their arms and legs fairly taut during the dive to support the top man and avoid his bumping, also to give better form (Fig. 3).   Topman ducks his head in close to Bottom's buttocks.   Bottom holds back mainly with his legs to ease the shock of the dive.   He must, however, bend his knees enough to allow his partner to roll in close. Topman continues the roll, pulling with his legs sufficiently to lift Bottom to his feet (Fig. 4).   The positions are now reversed, and one half has been made.

Bottom now goes up, down, and over; then Topman again, and so on.

The proper performance calls for a rhythmic series of counts: "Up, down, over," with about two seconds interval between each count. There should be no time lost between turns. Keep the rhythm of the counts from first to last of the series.

It will be difficult to keep your balance throughout, so proceed carefully and smoothly. Be sure that you jump up straight to form the "box," rather than out in front. The arms and legs must be kept straight for an easy balance. The shoulders and hips must be squarely on the mat. In lowering, the upper man should come

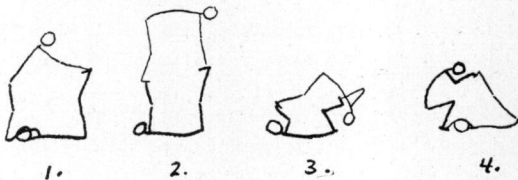

1.   2.   3.   4.

to an easy stand before diving. About three complete turns make a good series. End it by having Topman (Fig. 1) release Bottom's feet and dive through for an individual roll. Let Bottom follow with a snap-up.

It is not extremely difficult to take a "standing balance" (in Bottom's hands) from the box position (Fig. 2), pose for a moment, and then resume the high roll. This is an interesting variation. The count

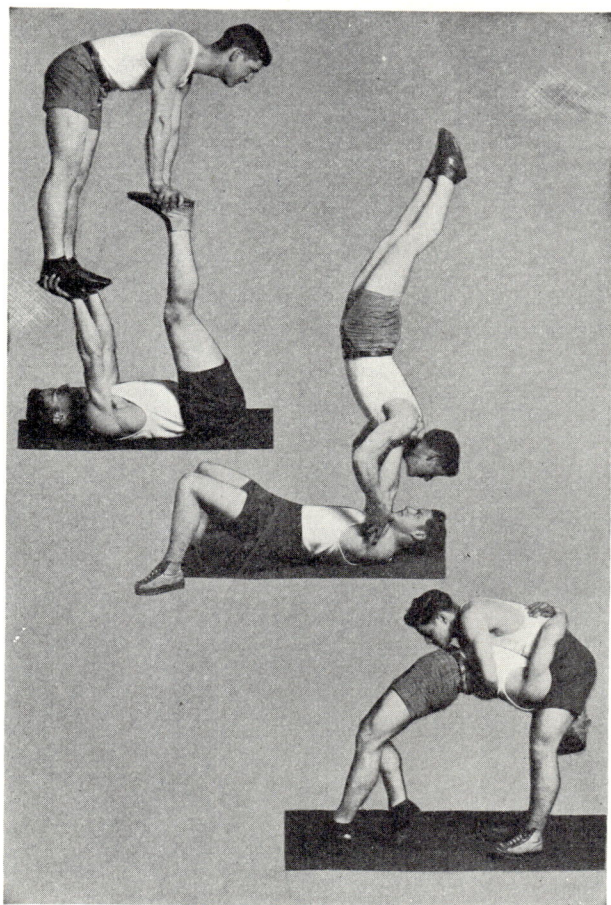

High roll—Shoulder stand—Double flip.

may be "up-stand-resume-down-over." Of course more time than two seconds must be allowed for the standing balance. Work it out for your best convenience.

SHOULDER STAND, SHIFT, DOWN, AND UP

Begin as for the shoulder balance (Fig. 1). When the performers are up in place let Topman shift, his weight forward, overbalancing very slightly in that direction, a little more on one side than on the other. Topman *shifts* the arm on this side, to the arm of Bottom, gripping him with the straight grip over the biceps just below the elbow. Topman's thumbs must be held rigidly, and the hand twisted around to the front, as far as convenient, to clamp the junction and counteract the overbalancing forward (Fig. 2). Then

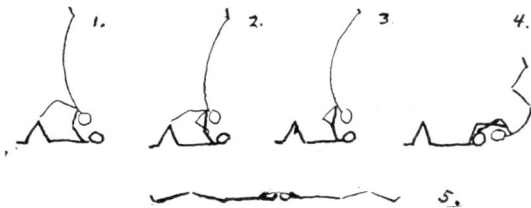

the weight is shifted a little more forward (especially on the other side this time) and Topman's other arm comes forward. This position is called the *shoulder stand* (Fig. 3). Topman merely gets in place and holds rigid. Bottom does all the balancing. The latter's arm are stretched out full length with the hands as near the tips of his partner's shoulders as possible.

From the shoulder stand Topman is dropped down on the mats behind Bottom to the position of Figure 4. From the position of Figure 3, Bottom slowly moves his arms up in the direction of his head until he can hold the weight no longer. Topman maintains equilibrium until Bottom breaks.

Then he ducks his head, rounds his shoulders, bends at the hips and leaves the leg flexible (Fig. 4). There is, of course, not a great deal of shock to this short fall. The doubling up process dissipates what little there is. After alighting, Topman stretches himself out full length, as does his partner, and the second part of the stunt is finished. They are *down* (Fig. 5).

In this position Bottom shifts his grip so that his hands are on Topman's biceps instead of on the shoulders. Also Topman's hands are on Bottom's biceps, Topman's arms are on the outside, while Bottom's are on the inside. They are ready for the jump now—to be *up* again. Topman rolls, jumping off the back of his head, very much as he would in doing the egg roll. Bottom is relaxed until the actual jump takes place. Then he jerks with all his strength toward the shoulder-stand position (Fig. 3). Topman should time his roll so that he will be slightly overbalanced forward as he lays out, and Bottom's pull will correct the balance.

Except that it is reversed and the grips are slightly changed, this coming *up* motion is exactly like the going down (Figs. 4 and 3). If Topman goes over *too far* on his roll up let him straighten or lay out a little sooner the next trial. If he doesn't get up *far enough* let him carry through a little farther with the roll and not lay out so soon.

The pose is held for a moment as before, then Topman lowers his legs to stand straddling Bottom's legs. Without loosening grips he picks Bottom up onto his feet, and the two stand facing each other.

The roll *up* may be done by either of the two partners. It is a much nicer stunt if they alternate. Remember, however, that in locking arms, those of the man to mount should be on the outside.

Shuttle or Triple Dive

This stunt is performed by three men. One stands an arm's length in front of another, both facing the third man who stands about two arms' lengths ahead of the first. The middle man, A (Fig. 1), does a forward roll, with his legs spread, toward B. B dives over between A's legs and completes a roll about where A started, just in front of the third man, C. C in turn dives through B's legs which are also spread and makes a roll where A first made his (Fig. 2). A, who by this time has got onto his feet, turns around quickly and dives over C, making a roll where B just made

8

one.   B has got onto his feet, turned around and is ready to dive over A again as A rolls.

This may go on indefinitely, each turning after his roll and diving again.   It usually does not, however, for someone is sure to fall into error before many turns have been completed.

In the diagrams X marks the spots where the men originally stood.   The figures in dotted lines show where the men in flight will roll.   In Figure 2, A is

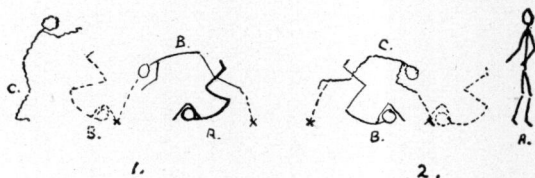

1.   *2.*

turning, and will be ready to dive when C is in the position suggested by the dotted lines.

Let each man remember to keep his legs apart, and to roll straight, as well as dive straight.   Let him get onto his feet and turn quickly.   The more speed the better the stunt appears.

To finish the stunt let A (Fig. 1) take two rolls and go off; and C, following him, take two, and go off.   B will have turned by then.   He has no one to dive over, but let him dive just the same, take two rolls and go off after the others.

The shuttle is a very enjoyable stunt; but be careful not to kick a partner in the face.

Monkey Roll

The monkey roll is similar in principle to the shuttle. The three men get down, side by side on all fours, with about three feet distance between each of them. The stunt is to be viewed from the front. Figure 1 shows side view to illustrate position. The other figures are front views. A rolls on his side to the left. As he does, B jumps over him, taking off from and alighting on all fours (Fig. 2). Immediately on alighting B rolls on his right side toward C. The latter jumps

1.   *2.*   *3.*

over him, and rolls toward A, who is on all fours again ready to jump. Figure 3 shows in solid line the figures at the start, and in dotted lines the courses they take.

This is an easier and funnier stunt than the shuttle. It is also faster.

A monkey roll may be ended the same as the shuttle. In turn, each man will roll twice toward the finish-end and go off.

For a funnier ending, let one man roll off, and the remaining two go over each other faster than before. Then have the second man go off, leaving the third man to himself rolling and hopping furiously. He may go so fast and wildly that he seems to be having a fit.

The others then run in, dive upon him and hold him still.
He stiffens, and they lift him by head and ankles like
a log, and carry him off.

Roll-up and Somersault

Bottom takes position as he would for planché: head
up, trunk erect, knees bent, feet apart, and well braced.
Topman runs in as he would for a handspring, but
instead of placing his hand on the mat, he puts them
on Bottom's knees, gripping straight and tightly (Fig.
1). Topman throws his feet up as in the handspring,
though not as hard. His arms are bent and his legs
slightly separated to fall easily over Bottom's shoulders
(straddling the neck) (Fig. 2). Bottom places his
hands under his partner's back and pushes up. Topman at the same time lifts his trunk by tightening his
abdominal muscles and comes up to a sitting position
on his partner's shoulders straddling his neck (Fig. 3).

1.   2.   3.   4.

They hold this pose a moment, juggle if necessary to
get set for the throw, then Topman throws his trunk
back; Bottom pushes up with both arms and legs.

This throws Topman off for a back somersault. He aids by jerking into a half-tucked position for the air turn and comes through nicely onto his feet standing (Fig. 4).

Be sure that you have your equilibrium at every point of the stunt. Don't go on, until you have perfect balance. At the start Bottom's knees must be bent enough to allow a good base for the handspring, and Topman must grip them tightly to avoid slipping down. As Topman's legs go over Bottom's shoulders, his mid-thighs should rest on the shoulders. On the throw back, Topman leads the motion and he must not forget to jerk on the tuck, to do his part in making the somersault. Bottom must exert himself for the powerful throw, pushing up and out. The higher the top man can be thrown the better.

Pull-up Mount

Two men stand facing each other with the cross-hand grip as for the step mount. Right hands are on top and twisted up, thumbs down. Bottom's feet are apart, the left slightly forward, and at an angle, well braced. Topman's feet are about a foot apart and astride the forward foot of his partner. Bottom leans over forward. Topman squats and lays his back on the mat (Fig. 1). Topman must be careful to squat close to his heels. This laying back is a wind-up. They are ready to throw.

The understander straightens up, both men pulling
in on the arms.   Topman is raised to his feet, still squat-
ting, as in the position of Figure 2.   From this position
he jumps straight up and with all his power.   Bottom

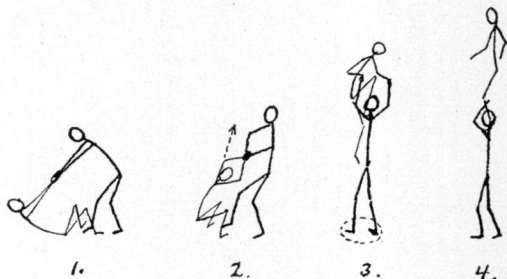

1.   *2.*   *3.*   *4.*

who has not slacked his pull from the beginning of the
throw carries through until his arms are over head.
He twists his back and changes his footing slightly.
The turn is through about 90 degrees so that his back
is to Topman.   Topman's left foot goes into position
first, on Bottom's left shoulder (Fig. 3), and the right
foot follows quickly onto Bottom's right shoulder.
From this squat position on Bottom's shoulders Topman rises to full height and the junction is clasped as for
regular two-high position (Fig. 4).

In learning this stunt you will find difficulty in holding
your balance.   Remember that all the action has to
take place over the small base covered by Bottom's feet
(dotted circle, Fig. 3).   Bottom, on the throw, must be
careful not to pull his partner back too far, so as to swing
him from over the base, and Topman must take care to

jump straight up, keeping over the base.   When Topman arrives on Bottom's shoulders the latter must have
his head up, back straight, and arms above his head.
The tendency is to pull the top man over forward.
Bottom can take as many steps as necessary to establish
and maintain equilibrium.   The fewer the better.

Handspring from Shoulders

[See illustration p. 120]

This stunt is begun from two-high position where
partners hold hands (Fig. 1).   Bottom stands staunchly
holding his arms rigid, though slightly bent.   Topman
throws his weight onto the arms, jumps a little from his
feet, ducks his head, rounds his back (contrary to true
handspring), and does a somersault over.   During the
somersault both men push on the arms.   Bottom
pushes with his legs as well (Fig. 2).   The grip is
released *after* the throw, and Topman takes his turn
in half-tuck position alighting upright on his feet.
The take-off is high, so Topman must hold back on his
spin, to keep from going over too far.   He also breaks
his tuck sooner.   Keep the eyes open.   This is an
interesting way to come down from two-high position.

Down and Over

This also is a good way to come down from two-high.
It is begun as the last stunt, from the position of Figure 1.
For the first move Topman merely jumps down close in

front of Bottom, letting his arms go behind him, holding
the grip (Fig. 3). Topman's wrists are bent and the
back of his hands are together. Bottom's wrists are
straight and so is his grip. Both have thumbs up.

Bottom begins the motion of the throw by swinging
the hands out, bending his knees and wrists so that he
can get his hands underneath, and push up on his
partner's arms. Topman springs and at the same time
acts against Bottom's push so that he is raised into the

1.   2.   3.   4.

air where he does a front somersault pushing from the
arms and half-tucking for his turn, just as on the hand-
spring-from-shoulders (Fig. 2). This is a difficult
stunt to do well, and a little dangerous. Be careful.
It is easier and safer, but inferior, when Topman does
not go very high for his turn (Fig. 4). Here Bottom
gives support, mostly by lifting instead of pushing up.
The stunt as first described is a stunt for experts. The
turn takes place above the underman's shoulders. In
the latter case, the turn takes place below his shoulders.
Try the latter first.

BELLY PITCH

Bottom lies on his back with his legs drawn up and relaxed. Topman stands with one foot beneath Bottom's buttocks and the other slightly back. He places, with his hands, the latter's feet on his upper abdominal wall. Bottom's feet should be together and the toes just over the lowest ribs of his partner. The partners grasp hands with straight forward grips (Fig. 1).

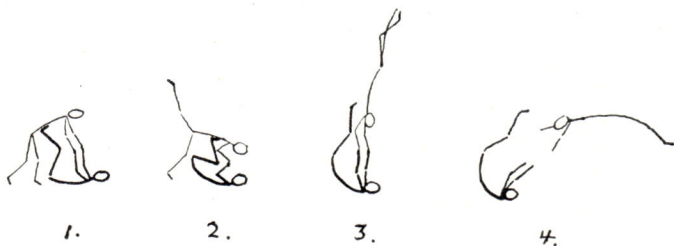

1.   2.   3.   4.

As a wind-up, Topman pulls back, tightening the arms and lifting Bottom's shoulders a little. The latter presses lightly with his legs so as to keep good contact with Topman's belly.

From this position Topman begins the throw, by plunging forward throwing his weight onto Bottom's feet and starting to flip. The arms are drawn in and one foot goes up as in the handspring (Fig. 2). In fact, this stunt is a handspring. As Topman flips over, Bottom gives a vigorous kick which sends Topman flying. At the same moment Topman gets a good handspring push from the arms which adds still more force to the throw (Fig. 3). He sails high into the air, lying out completely like a reverse swan dive (Fig. 4).

The belly pitch calls for delicate timing and cooperation. When it is done correctly you will be astonished at the tremendous height and distance the man on top flies. He must keep his eyes open, and be careful not to go over too far.

The arm movement is important. Bottom especially must hold up on his arms and give a good throw when the right moment arrives. The push comes a fraction of a second after the kick; both should be directed straight up.

Topman's course of flight should be up over an arch as in the dive. His feet at the beginning of flight point almost straight up. He must be careful about bringing them down too soon; he may go over too far, onto his face.

Variation: The next diagram shows several other pitches from nearly the same position.

Figure 1 illustrates a belly pitch wherein Topman grasps Bottom's ankles. The motions of the throw are the same, except that Topman gets his arm-push from Bottom's legs instead of from Bottom's arms. The push is important, nevertheless, and must not be omitted. Timing is about the same and the throw just as good in the two stunts.

STRADDLE PITCH

Bottom draws up his legs farther than for the two preceding stunts, curling his back until his feet are straight over him.   Topman stands astride, facing in the direction he will travel, with Bottom's feet beneath his crotch

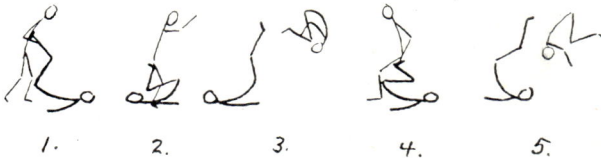

1.   2.   3.   4.   5.

(Fig. 2).   Topman begins the throw by rising on his toes and slinging his arms up; then he bends and takes off as for a front somersault.   Bottom kicks, at the moment of the jump, adding force to the jump and making the front somersault possible.   The tuck and landing are the same as described under front somersault.

SEAT PITCH

[See Illustration above]

Positions at starting are the same as for straddle pitch, except that Topman stands at Bottom's buttocks instead of astride, and places Bottom's feet on his seat instead of in his crotch (Fig. 4).   The somersault is a back instead of a front somersault, so the throw is backward, and the flight is over Bottom in the direction of his head (Fig. 5).   Topman begins the motion by jumping up slightly back, and turning a somersault. The business of Topman rising on his toes before the throw is good as a wind-up and important as a signal to Bottom.   The technic of the throw is like that of the back somersault, except that the tuck is not tight and the turn slower.   It is desirable for Topman to go almost straight up and to alight just behind the shoulders of his partner.   His feet should be slightly apart on landing, and care should be taken to avoid stepping on Bottom.

Topman may find it easier in learning to keep hold of his partner's feet during the throw (Fig. 4).   Later, he should be able to turn straight without this aid.

HANDSTAND ROLL

Bottom stands erect facing in the direction the pair will travel.   Topman is about three feet behind him,

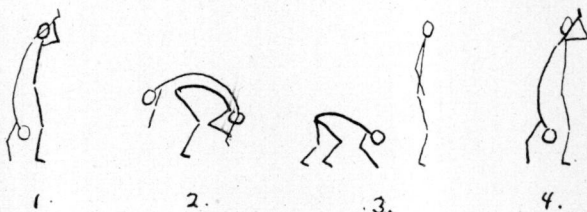

1.   2.   .3.   4.

with one foot ahead of the other.   Topman stoops, places his hands about eighteen inches behind Bottom's heels, and throws a handstand letting his legs fall on Bottom's shoulders (Fig. 1).   Bottom grasps his partner's ankles, stoops forward and places Topman's feet on the floor (Fig. 2).

The positions are now reversed. Topman stands erect and Bottom throws the handstand (Figs. 3 and 4).

In throwing the handstand Bottom must take care to throw just enough to get into the position of Figure 1. He must not strike his partner with such force as to move him from his tracks. His legs should be spread slightly to straddle the neck.

If a series of such handstands are done quickly, smoothly, and with rhythm, the effect is very pleasing. Beginners sometimes do this stunt but it takes advanced tumblers to do it well.

Neckbreaker

Topman stands with his legs apart and back to the direction he will be thrown. Bottom, just behind him,

1.   *2.*   *3.*   *4.*

stoops and places his own head between Topman's legs. Bottom's feet are well apart, one slightly ahead of the other. His hands are on his knees, elbows out. Topman holds on to Bottom's shoulders to steady himself (Fig. 1).

Topman rises on his toes as a wind-up, then throws back as Bottom, straightening up, lifts him off the ground (Fig. 2). Bottom's motion is chiefly extending his arms and back. The force is exerted through his neck. It is by means of the neck that Topman is thrown—hence the name.

Topman should spring from his feet as he is lifted. His arms on Bottom's shoulders serve to steady him, and also give a little push as he goes clear into the air. He should not tuck, but bend at the hips as illustrated (Figs. 3 and 4). The underman's throw must be quick and powerful. A strong underman can throw to considerable height. Keep your eyes open.

In learning this stunt a third man may be of considerable help if he places his hand on the shoulder of the man to be thrown, and steadies him during the air-turn. Danger is entirely removed if two men, one on each side, lend this aid.

KIP OFF BACK

Bottom stands well braced with legs bent and hands on knees. His back is straight, not rounded, and inclined at an angle of 45 degrees. His arms are very slightly bent and his head is ducked forward as much as possible (Fig. 1).

Topman runs in, places his hands on his partner's hips, and does a sort of dive roll onto Bottom's back and shoulder (Fig. 2). As his shoulders touch Bot-

Three men pyramid.

tom's, Bottom "gives" slightly (Fig. 3), then pushes forcibly up, straightening his legs (even to jumping) and rounding his shoulders. Topman reacts to this boost by sailing into the air in lay-out position. His movements at this part of the throw are similar to those of the snap-up or kip (Figs. 3 and 4).

1.   2.   3.   4.

It is very difficult to adjust timing in this stunt. It will take considerable practice for Bottom to learn just when to push. Topman must be careful to place his shoulders on Bottom's shoulders, not in the middle of his back. Topman should take off from both feet very close to Bottom, so that his dive will be up and down instead of too much forward, which would upset Bottom.

Bottom may not be able to assume the right angle with back straight unless Topman directs him. Experiment a little with the inclination.

Since Bottom cannot see his partner, Topman should call "ready" as he starts to run. The preliminary count comes when hands are placed, and the executory count as shoulders touch.

9

A throw which comes too late will tend to throw
Topman over too far; one which comes too soon, not
far enough.

Bottom bends over as for the neckbreaker, hands on
knees, elbows out. Topman walks in from the direction Bottom faces, places his hands on Bottom's
elbows and throws a leg over Bottom's neck, thus
straddling (Fig. 1). As his leg touches and his weight

1.   2.   3.   4.

is shifted, he bends in the knees, Bottom "giving"
with him (Fig. 2). This is the preliminary movement.
After taking the preliminary count, the throw follows
immediately.

Bottom straightens up forcibly with the executory
count as for the neckbreaker, but keeps his arms bent
and pushes considerably with them (Fig. 3). Topman
handsprings from Bottom's elbows and flies high into
the air for a lay-out somersault (Fig. 4).

When Topman throws his leg over Bottom's neck,
the movement should be in the same rhythm as Top-

man's walking.   No time should be lost in this motion.
The bend and pitch should follow immediately.   The
pitch seems to be one long motion, but as in the belly-
pitch, there are two parts: the jump and the handspring.   There must be no hitch in between.   The
handspring immediately follows the jump, and they
flow into each other as a single motion.

In learning, the beginner had better start from
standing straddle position (Fig. 2).   Someone can
steady Topman by placing a hand on his shoulder.   He
must get a good push from the arms, in the handspring,
if he is to reach full height in flying.

One Leg Back

Bottom stands solidly with feet separated and hands
ready to receive Topman's leg.   The latter walks in
from the side, places one hand on his partner's shoulder,
raises his inside leg and places it in Bottom's hands.
Bottom holds the legs from the under side, one hand
beneath the heel, the other beneath the knee (Fig. 1).
Topman rises on his toes and jumps from one leg
straight up into the air, as in the back somersault.   As
he jumps, Bottom lifts hard on the other leg (Fig. 2).
When Topman reaches the height of his jump he rears
back on the leg which Bottom is lifting.   This causes
him to spin with a zip.   The height gained by the jump
and lift allows amply for a lay-out somersault and a full
standing finish (Figs. 3 and 4).

Bottom's work is chiefly lifting. But he must be prepared to resist the vigorous kick which comes on the lay-out. There must be no recoil whatever on his part when Topman throws for the spin. His lifting motion should follow all the way through, not stop at shoulder height (Fig. 3).

Topman should jump to full height before attempting to go over backwards. The height is most important. When he reaches the peak, he rears back, throwing all

1.   2.   3.   4.

his weight and strength onto the inside leg. Bottom's hold gives a resistance from which comes the spin. The arms go up on the jump at take-off, but are drawn to the side on the lay-out (Figs. 2 and 3).

In beginning you might find it easier to start from a stand (Fig. 1). If you start with the walk-in, no time should be lost after lifting the leg before jumping. The counts "ready—allez-opp!" should fall respectively as Topman puts his hand on the shoulder, places his leg, and throws. Placing the leg should be a clear-cut distinct motion, and a little wind-up dip should follow immediately—all during the count "allez." This walk-in is of course a much better beginning from the standpoint of showmanship.

It is rather easy to do a half-twist on the end of the somersault.   In fact, when you get a good high throw, it is difficult to keep from doing one.   (Half-twists will be described in the next chapter.)

CHUTE PICK-UP

Topman lies on his back on the mat with his feet in the direction he will travel.   Bottom grasps his hands

1.   2.   3.   4.

and stands just behind Topman's shoulders, right foot slightly ahead of the left (Fig. 1).

On the preliminary signal Bottom pulls back on Topman's arms; as a wind-up on the executory signal, with legs wide apart, he takes three quick steps to a position astride Topman and slightly ahead of him. He is bent over, arms between legs.   Topman by this time has drawn in his legs, as for a tuck, and is ready to be pitched (Fig. 2).

Bottom pitches his partner by lifting and pulling forward.   Topman must be in such a position that his whole body weight can be lifted and swung by arms alone. As Bottom pulls and lifts, Topman swings through Bottom's legs, and breaks tuck by shooting his own legs up toward the ceiling (Fig. 3). Bottom continues to pull with his arms and back muscles until Topman is pitched into the air, where he arches into a reverse swan, and comes down fully standing (Fig. 4).

This is a smooth, beautiful stunt. It calls for close cooperation, and delicate balancing, especially by Topman. He must handle his body in such a way that one pull from Bottom will lift him clear of the mats and allow him to swing. As he swings through the legs he must skilfully open his tuck in such a way as to fly up and out. He pulls with his own arms as he opens tuck to increase the force of the throw.

Topman does not double up until Bottom jumps astride him. The three steps of Bottom which comprise this jump are short and quick. They should bring his feet alongside the spot where Topman's knees were when extended. The arms during this time are, of course, relaxed. The real pull does not come until after the position of Figure 2 has been reached. It should be long and forceful though slow. Bottom must carry through the throw to the position of Figure 4, and Topman must be careful not to drop his feet too soon. The course of flight is up and down over an arch. However, the curve is sharper than for the dive.

Heel Pick-up

Topman sits on the mat in close tuck position. His partner stands a little in front of him, legs apart. Bottom stoops over, reaches through his legs, and grasps Topman's heels (Fig. 1). To throw, Bottom straightens up, pulling forward and lifting to swing Topman through his legs, as in the last stunt. Topman holds tightly to his tuck during this swing (Fig. 2). When the position of Figure 2 is reached, Bottom

1.   2.   3.   4.

throws Topman's heels down, causing him to spin over as in a back somersault. Topman opens the tuck as he spins over and alights half crouched (Fig. 4). Throughout this stunt Topman is always close to the mat. His tuck must be tight and the spin quick in order for him to get over onto his feet. He may find it rather difficult to hold his legs in when his whole weight is suspended by them; but the tuck must be held tightly until he is over almost onto his feet. Bottom should be careful to lift his partner high enough before the spin to preclude the possibility of Topman's head striking the floor.

ARMPIT PICK-UP

Topman lies on his back, gripping hands with his partner as in the chute pick-up. Bottom stands in close to his shoulders (Fig. 1). Topman begins the motion by rolling back and throwing his legs under the arms of his partner, who has leaned over to make this possible. Bottom's arms should cross Topman's thighs

1.   2.   3.   4.

just above the knees (Fig. 2). As soon as Topman's legs are under, Bottom begins to straighten up and they both pull with the arms. Topman's legs are fixed so his body is lifted like a lever toward the upright position (Fig. 3). The lifting is done with a throw so that Topman may swing high enough to drop gracefully onto his feet (Fig. 4). Bottom tries to get under Topman at the peak of this swing so as to support Topman's weight by the arms, have better control, and let him down easily. The back muscles of both men do the most important work of this stunt.

BIRD LIFT

Bottom stands with his feet apart, one a little ahead of the other. His knees are slightly bent, and he is well

Bird lift.

braced to receive a jolt from the front.   Topman runs in until he is about two feet in front of Bottom, who places his hands on Topman's hips just at the crest of the ilium.   Topman's hands are slapped on Bottom's shoulders (Fig. 1).   Without hesitation, and using the force of the run, Topman jumps almost straight up, as

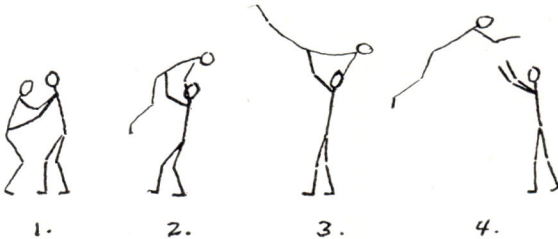

1.   2.   3.   4.

high as he can, lifting his feet and lowering his head as in a dive (Fig. 2).   Bottom gets underneath him and raises the latter part of his body by pushing up on the hips. Topman arches his back and stiffens his arms, assuming the position pictured in Figure 3.   This is a pose.   In adagio dancing it is done without Topman's using his arms either for gaining position or balancing.   However the person on top is nearly always a woman.   Men's shoulders are heavier and the arms can be employed to good advantage—especially when the two performers are near the same weight.

In breaking the pose Bottom throws Topman forward, onto his feet (Fig. 4).   Topman can give a nice finishing touch to the stunt by doing a backward roll as he goes down onto the mat.

In mounting let Topman remember to jump from close in, and straight up. Bottom must be careful to place his hands just on the corners of the boney girdle of the hips. If they are placed too high he may not be able to lift Topman into place; if too low, Topman tends to go over behind him spoiling the balance. Bottom will need to have strong arms in order to make the push which lifts Topman into final position. Almost all of the weight is supported by his arms alone. Topman will face a tendency to bend at the hips and arms when he thinks he is going over too far. He must hold the arch rigidly. Bottom can keep Topman from falling in any event, if he does not let go his grip on the hips.

This stunt may well be used as a unit in the more difficult pyramids.

Double Roll Over Back

Topman lies on his belly, legs extended and separated. Bottom backs up in between them, catches hold of the ankles and lifts Topman's crotch up onto the top of his own hips (Fig. 1). Then bending forward he pushes down on Topman's legs, which are held stiff. At the same time Topman arches his back and is raised to the vertical position astride Bottom's back (Fig. 2). Bottom follows through with the push on the legs far enough to put Topman in a position from which he may roll backwards over Bottom's shoulders onto his feet (Figs. 3 and 4).

As far as the throw is concerned position shown in Figure 1 is the starting point.   Bottom's bend forward and push down are done with force.   Topman, acting against this motion, is thrown sharply up.   If he uses this force advantageously he will be able to roll easily and prettily over his partner's shoulders onto the mats beyond.

1.   2.   3.   4.

When Topman's weight rests directly on Bottom's shoulders, Bottom gives a bounce upwards as in the kip off back, which adds height to Topman's air-turn and makes the stunt a little more spectacular.

This stunt can be done slowly as well as fast.   In learning try to work it slowly first.

ONE LEG FRONT

The two partners stand facing in the same direction, Bottom about 18 inches behind Topman, with his hands on Topman's hips.   Topman places his own hands on Bottom's hands to be able to feel the starting signal (Fig. 1).   Bottom begins by calling "Ready," stooping, and grasping Topman's right foot which has been raised for the purpose. In gripping, Bottom's left hand goes beneath Topman's ankle and his right hand beneath Topman's toes. As soon as the stunt is begun by Bottom removing hands from Topman's hips, Topman lifts his right leg, handles his arms as for the front somersault, and is ready to throw. Bottom at the same time steps back slightly with the right foot, takes

1.   2.   3.   4.

his grip, bends a little also (Fig. 2). All this is on the preliminary, or first count. On the executory, or second count, Topman jumps high into the air, aided by a lift from his partner and is thrown for a front somersault. Topman's take-off and flight are the same as for the regular front somersault only he relies chiefly on the push he can get from the leg his partner holds for the force of his throw. He must try to get a great deal of height from the jump and the lift before he tucks for the spin. Bottom must lift quickly and with great force. He should follow through to a point shoulder-high before quitting his throw (Figs. 3 and 4).

A pleasing, but more difficult, way to enter this stunt is for Topman, facing Bottom, to walk in and place his foot as for a pitchback (see page 167, Fig. 1). But in an extra count before the throw let him twist to the left (as in tour jeté), standing all the while on the ball of his left foot, until he is in the position of Figure 2, from which the stunt proceeds in due order. Bottom, of course, must let the foot turn in his hands during this twist.

To make it still more fancy let Topman enter as for pitchback, place his foot, and then stand a moment in Bottom's hands during which time he puts his own hands on Bottom's head and passes his left leg completely over Bottom's head, twisting to the right as he does in order to bring it down again to stand on (Fig. 2), and jump from. This part of the stunt is done slowly and with careful attention to balance. Topman must be in perfect equilibrium before he undertakes the somersault (Figs. 3 and 4).

CHAPTER IX

TUMBLING FOR EXPERTS—INDIVIDUAL

The stunts of this chapter and the one to follow are entirely within the range of good amateur tumblers. They are, nevertheless, the type of stunts seen on the professional stage and in the circus ring. Only those performers who have shown especially good talent with the less difficult stunts are expected to try these. A belt should be handy and at least two thicknesses of mats as safeguards during the learning period.

The descriptions of this chapter are addressed to the proficient worker, the expert. They are therefore less detailed, and more suggestive. An understanding of the technic of all the stunts which have gone before is assumed.

Back Dive Slap

Stand and dip just as for back-handspring (Figs. 1 and 2). On the throw bend your back more and place your hands further under you (Fig. 3). Receive most of the shock on your arms; then drop to your chest, and rock down (Figs. 4 and 5). Be careful to get a good arch and try to let your legs drag behind as much as possible, so the slap will not be too severe.   Do not double your toes under; slap with the top of your foot (Fig. 5).

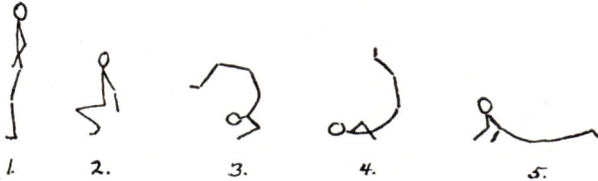

Finish this stunt as you would an egg-roll, coming to a full stand.

CRADLE

Begin with a snap-up (Figs. 1 and 2).   Then reverse the movement exactly, diving back to the original position on the mat (Figs. 3, 4, and 5).   This repeated several times without a pause and in smooth rhythm is called the cradle.

After reaching a stand with the snap-up, dip as for back handspring, (Fig. 3), and dive *up* over an arch. Most beginners fail to dive *up* and to open and tuck, thereby causing a bad bump.   Don't forget to have the arms extended well out ahead of you to receive most of the shock of the dive (Fig. 4).   The head should be bent forward slightly just as the hands touch, and part of the shock received on the back of the neck and shoulders, chiefly shoulders.   Another portion of

10

the shock is dissipated in the movement of doubling
to the position of Figure 5.

1.   2.   3.   4.   5.

Make the points where hands and feet touch fairly
close together.   And on the dive, remember to go up,
over an arch.   Do not lose any time between dive and
kip.

BACK HANDSPRING WITH HALF-TWIST

Begin the handspring as normally (Fig. 1).   After
the spring when you push off with your arm, bring down

1.   2.   3.   4.

the left foot as usual, but let the right drag behind, and
with it start to twist the whole body to the right.   This
twist starts at the bottom and works up toward the
head-end.   It is performed mostly after the left foot
hits and before the upright position is gained (Figs. 2
and 3).   It must be done quickly, and the second handspring in an opposite direction undertaken immediately.

Four or five of these done in quick series gives an impression of whirling, graceful beauty. When done by experts, the twist is completed always before the right foot touches, and before the upright position is gained. Thus the angle the body makes with the floor is always less than 90 degrees (Fig. 4). The twist is pivoted on the ball of the left foot. Don't forget to dip before throwing each hand-spring.

Standing Front Somersault

Stand erect, your weight on the toes, and arms outstretched in front of you (Fig. 1). Dip sharply but

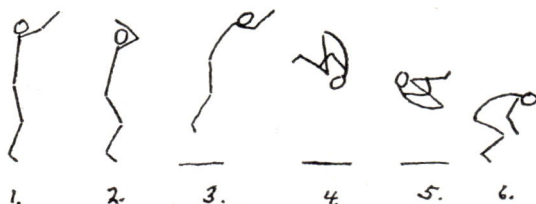

very little (Fig. 2), and take off as you would for the running somersault, but without the run (Fig. 3). You will find it necessary to act much more quickly, and lean forward slightly. The tuck must be entered with extreme rapidity and held very close. However, do not jeopardize your jump by tucking too soon. A powerful spring is necessary to give the proper height.

Do not fail to use your arms. They play an important part in the upward motion of the take-off (Figs.

2 and 3), and in the downward motion of the throw for tucking (Fig. 4).

When learning do not try to open your tuck at all. Alight completely balled up. As you become more proficient, open out sooner (Fig. 6). Some performers do a full layout somersault from standing position. Many tuck, and alight upright. Nevertheless, it is an unusual accomplishment to get over at all, even without opening your tuck.

Round-off

The round-off is not much of a stunt by itself but it works nicely in with other stunts and is one of the best wind-ups for air-turns. It is essentially a front hand-spring with a half-twist.

Run in as for the handspring. When you throw the arms up, let the left arm go higher than the right (Fig. 1). As you bend down for the throw, touch the mat only with the left arm. Swing the right on through and around behind you in a complete circle. You will find it necessary to swing the right arm down a little sooner in order to do this (Fig. 2).

As you kick up with the left foot, twist the whole body a half-turn to the right, throwing yourself sidewise for the central position as in the cartwheel (Fig. 3). This twisting motion is usually led by the arm swinging around and turning the shoulders onto the side. The right hand, after swinging over the head, is placed on the mat about a foot ahead of the other, and at right angles to the direction of travel. The left hand was placed at a 45 degree angle. The right is slightly to the left of the line, to allow for the twist (Fig. 6). Both hands turn a little in their tracks as the last phase of the stunt is executed.

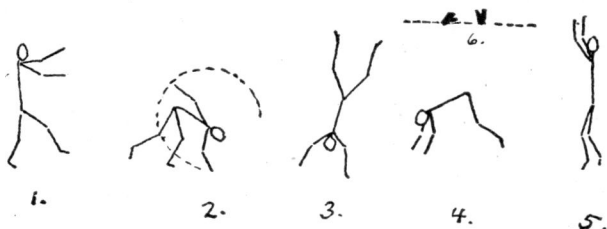

Once having begun the twist carry through without a break. From the inverted position (Fig. 3), pull the legs down sharply, completing the half-twist. At the same time push up on the hands as in the back handspring (Fig. 4). This throws you onto your feet facing the direction from which you started. The finish is exactly like that of the back handspring (Fig. 5).

Run in straight; do not swerve for the twist. Keep your shoulders squared forward until the first hand touches. When running, be up on your toes, step lightly, and let your arms be flexible—only during the run, however. When you throw do it with zip! Keep your body up as high as possible while you are turning, up on your fingertips even, as in the handspring.

The round-off is a flip rather than a jump. Your body spins around a hub; it does not leap.

You will find it difficult, but essential, to get your turn and twist together smoothly. Twisting must not throw you out of the single vertical plane in which you travel.

When your legs come together and you pull down for the finish, use all your strength—"whip" the legs down so that your feet hit the mat with a bang! If you are to do another stunt with the round-off this "whipping" is very important. It gives the speed and momentum you'll need.

Round-off Back Handspring

This, as the name implies, is a combination of round-off and back handspring. If you can do the two stunts separately you should be able to do them in series. It is not so easy to put them together as logic would lead you to believe. You need to be more than a mathematician, or a logician. In fact you must be a pretty good tumbler. Have a couple of men stand ready to spot you when you first try.

Do the round-off in the orthodox fashion, but do not jump high at the end (Figs. 1 and 2). Instead let your momentum carry you until you are a little overbalanced backwards (Fig. 3), and then throw for the handspring. You will have great speed and considerable force from the momentum of the round-off, which make the stunt doubly beautiful, and the necessity for getting each movement correct doubly important.

Avoid jumping high as you enter the handspring, and be ready to receive a good shock on your arms as you dive. Arch your back a great deal, and whip your legs over with force. As you flip, bring your feet down with a bang, and jump into the air for a finish.

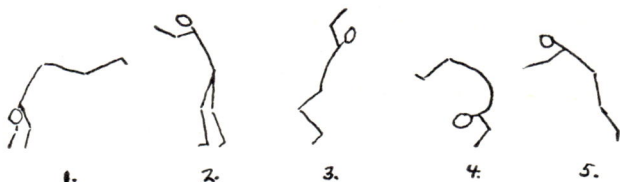

1.   **2.**   **3.**   **4.**   **5.**

The combination is even more wonderful, if you add on the end a back somersault. It comes rather easily after the quick handspring, and a great height is possible. This combination is called the "triple flash."

Smoothness and speed are keynotes to directions for these combinations.

Round-off Back Somersault

The approach is quite the same as for the preceding stunt. Get all the force possible into the whip from your round-off. Hit the mats hard, and jump into the air (Figs. 1, 2, 3, 4). There is no halt between round-off and jump for the somersault. The arms should come up directly from the mats to throw for the somersault.

The angle the line of the body makes with the horizontal is rather important. The diagram shows the correct inclination for consecutive positions throughout the stunt. Jump straight up. The momentum of the round-off will carry you back considerably. The arms play an important part in the take-off. Be sure to use them. Provided the round-off is good, an astounding height may be reached in jumping for the somersault. The author turns somersaults as high as six

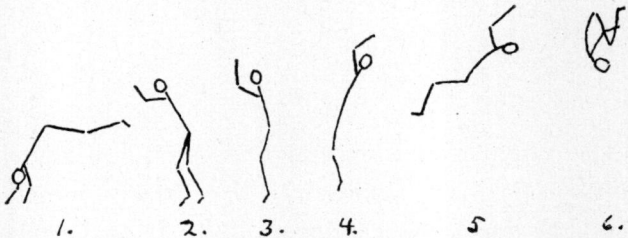

feet above the mats. Get your height before you tuck (Fig. 5), and break your tuck in time to keep from going over too far. Keep your eyes open, by all means.

Be careful in learning this stunt. Have at least one good spotter stand by to assist in case of need. Three or four helpers are not superfluous.

Again let me emphasize the importance of smoothness and speed.

Round-off Back Lay-out Somersault

This is the same as the preceding stunt except that the body is extended and arched during the somersault.

Side somersault.

It is nearly a compromise between the two preceding stunts.

It requires an exceptionally good round-off and a high jump. Arms go up on the take-off (Fig. 3), but come to the side about the middle of the somersault— or rather the torso comes to them (Fig. 4).

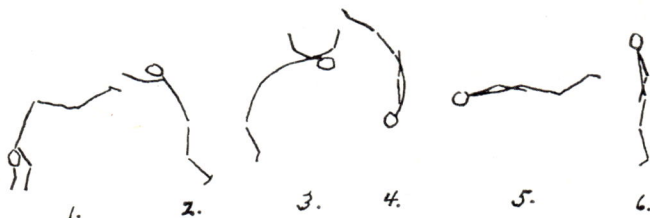

1.   2.   3.   4.   5.   6.

Getting height is the chief problem. The lay-out somersault must be high enough above the mats to allow you to alight fully standing (Fig. 6). The knees and hips are bent slightly just before landing to better receive the shock and to facilitate balance. Arch well and point your toes during flight. This is one of the most beautiful stunts a tumbler can do.

Round-off Side Somersault

The round-off here is unorthodox. It is a cross between a true round-off and a tinsica. It is finished with feet on a line pointing in the direction you travel. One foot hits after the other, and on the take-off for the somersault one leaves the mat before the other. In this respect the take-off is similar to that in cart-

wheels with jumps.   The jump is straight up, and must
be high.   The turning seems rather slow as compared
with that of the other stunts.

The side somersault is just what the name implies.
You take off from the rear (right) foot, first throwing
the corresponding arm high on that side at the same
time, and throwing from the other foot immediately
after.   The body should be bent and inclined toward
the direction you will turn (Fig. 1).   You can effect a
tuck by drawing the legs in and slapping the arms—the
left particularly—against the thighs (Fig. 2).   The tuck
is not close; angles at knees and hips are almost right
angles.   You break tuck, and alight still facing the

1.   *2.*   *3.*   *4.*   *5.*

side (Figs. 3 and 4).   You may stop here, or make a
turn to the left, after alighting, and continue the run.
This stunt is quite unique and effective.   It may be
done in full lay-out, which is at once a more difficult and
more effective performance.

If you make a half twist to the right while turning the
somersault, you will come down facing the starting
point, and will have done a "baroni."   This will not
be very difficult after you have learned the side somer-

sault.   All you need do is to get good height on the jump, and turn the head sharply to the right in the middle of the somersault.   The rest takes care of itself.

You can also do a quarter twist in the other direction, so as to alight in the position of Figure 5, by turning the head to the left while in flight.   However, this twist is more difficult.   In all these stunts the legs must be given a good flip on the take-off so that they will carry over properly.

Tinsica

This is a forward handspring in which you take off from one foot after the other, and from one hand after

1.   2.   3 .   4.   5.

the other.   Run in as for handspring, only have the right arm held higher than the left.   (The left foot is forward, Fig. 1.)   You throw just as for the handspring except that the right hand is placed about 18 inches ahead of the left and that the feet are not brought together in the air.   The kick-up must be very forceful —one foot after the other.   The push from the hands is also one after the other.   The back must be arched greatly (Figs. 2 and 3).

The performer's hands should leave the mat before his feet touch, as in the handspring, but since his arms and legs are separated, the time he is in the air is considerably less. On alighting, right foot touches first, and should go way under, not much more than 24 inches ahead of where the right hand was placed (Fig. 3). The left foot comes down immediately after, about 18 inches ahead of the right. The push from the arms and the momentum of the flip should throw you easily onto your feet and into a position from which you may continue running (Fig. 4).

The instructions given under handspring and round-off about keeping up high on toes and fingers, throwing sharply, etc., all apply here.

Tinsica-front Somersault

[See Illustration, p. 157]

Do the tinsica as just directed. When you reach the upright position (Figs. 4 and 5), do not stop but leap right into a front somersault. The take-off will be from the position of Figure 5 with legs separated. The arms are up already so the force of the throw comes chiefly from the legs. Some, of course, comes from the momentum gained in the tinsica. Be sure that you are well over onto your feet after the tinsica before you take-off for the somersault. The jump from the legs for the somersault should be forceful; the tuck, quick and close. Keep the eyes open. Figure out mentally just

how you will turn, and watch yourself.   Keep high up
on fingertips and toes.   This is not an easy stunt.

GAINER

When one does a back somersault and alights in the
tracks from which he took-off, he does a "spotter."   If
he alights ahead of his tracks he does a "gainer."

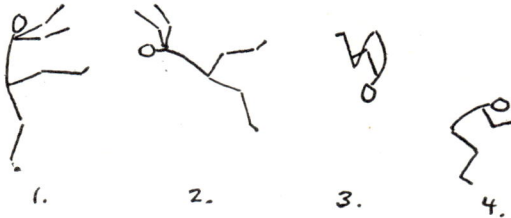

The throw is very much like punting a football,
though more attention is given the ground leg than the
raised leg (Fig. 1), and the arms are thrown up forcibly
as in the back somersault.   It is a take-off from one leg,
and therefore quite difficult.   Walk in slowly, facing
forward, body erect.   Get a good jump, throw the head
back quickly (Fig. 2), and tuck close (Fig. 3).   When
you have perfected this stunt you will come down in
such a way that you can continue your run forward
(Fig. 4).   It is simply a back somersault done from a
forward run.

BACK SOMERSAULT WITH HALF-TWIST

In order to do twisters you must have exceptional
height to your jumps.   Therefore, the twists are usually

done in combination with round-off, back handspring, or some other stunt which allows great height.

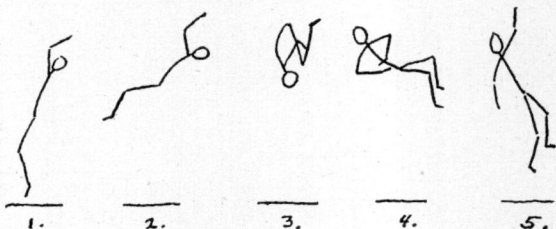

Take your somersault as usual, without thinking of the twist until you break your tuck. Then jerk the head sharply to the right or left, swinging the arms in that direction also. This turns the body easily and you have merely to follow through with the twist progressing from head to foot to do a nice job of the stunt. Since the twist takes place in the interval between opening tuck and alighting, the tuck must be broken early and high, and the twist must be quick.

Have someone stand beside the mat, and call at the proper moment to break. When you hear the call jerk your head to the side and look at the helper. If you are high enough, you will be surprised how easily you turn.

Be sure to begin the twist with the head and not with the feet.

FRONT SOMERSAULT AND HALF-TWIST

Again it is necessary to have exceptional height, which is not so easy to get with a front somersault.

Four men pyramid.

As an individual performance this stunt is limited to a small group of tumblers who have remarkable strength in their legs. All of the twists fit better in combination with companion stunts where greater height on the throws is possible. However, the twists themselves are individual stunts.

Run in as for simple somersault. Jump as high as you can; break tuck early, and twist as you are coming down. The directions for twisting are exactly the same as given in the preceding stunt: jerk the head and arms to the side as you break your tuck. Alight upright.

Front Lay-out Somersault

This is a front somersault in full lay-out position.

Run in as for the dive handspring. Take off in the same manner, but with greater force, to allow greater

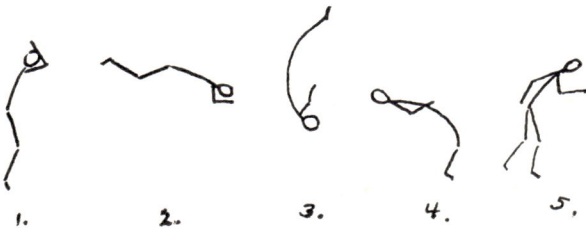

height. The hands are above the shoulders on the jump. They must be slung forcibly down and out to the side (Figs. 1, 2, and 3). The feet are thrown high at the take-off and the head low. In the inverted lay-out position (Fig. 3), the head will sometimes be within 18 inches of the mat, and yet the performer comes out standing. As you rise at the take-off the knee and hip joints are bent slightly. The full lay-out is not gained until almost the midpoint of the turn. Later when you are nearly all the way over bend slightly at the knees to facilitate landing (Fig. 4). The arch of your back, once attained, should be maintained throughout.

The most difficult part of the stunt is the leg work. To begin with you must get a tremendous jump; then flip your feet high and fast. They pass through a bigger arc than does your head. In fact, the turning hub is at about the center of your breast, instead of the navel, as for the handsprings. This is really a very difficult stunt.

When you learn it—if you do—try a half-twist in combination.

CHAPTER X

TUMBLING FOR EXPERTS—COMPANION

TRIPLE ROLL OR CATERPILLAR

THIS is on the order of the simple double roll, but three men take part instead of two. C lies on his back, legs drawn up. B also lies on his back in a line with C, his head between C's legs, and his hands gripping C's ankles, as in double roll. A stands at C's shoulders, and grasps with his hands B's ankles which have been raised for the purpose, requiring B to curl up on his back as in the kip wind-up (Fig. 1). The grips in every case are straight forward, and the partners are just about as close together as they can be.

1.　　　　　*2.*　　　　　*3.*

A starts the motion by diving over (Fig. 2), and rolling in close between B's legs which are drawn up as A comes down. The force of A's dive pulls C, who is hanging on to A's ankles, up to a stand. Thus each man has moved up one position (Fig. 3). A is now in

front, **B** in the middle, and **C** standing. **D** dives and
rolls in a similar fashion, and each man moves up
another position. The stunt is a continuous process
of this diving and rolling.

Let each man remember to dive in close to the man
beneath him. Everyone must hold muscles of the
arms and legs fairly taut as the top man goes over in
order to support his weight evenly, and have good
control of the caterpillar. This does not mean to hold
arms and legs straight. The knees and elbows both
must be fully flexed while on the mats and partly
flexed while in the air. Be careful not to stretch out too
long, and take your time. You can do the stunt as well
slowly as fast.

PITCHBACK

Bottom stands very solid with legs apart, toes pointing obliquely out, knees bent, but torso vertical. He
places his left hand in his right hand (both palms up)
and grasps the thumb of the left with the thumb and
forefinger of the right, thus locking the hands together.
His elbows are in to his sides touching the crests of the
ilium. The pocket of his hands protrudes three or
four inches out in front of his navel. This allows a
good purchase for Topman's foot which is to be placed
in the hands.

Topman walks in, lays his hands on Bottom's shoulders, and places one foot in the pocket of Bottom's

hands (Fig. 1). To throw they both dip slightly, and Topman jumps straight up, getting his push from both legs but chiefly from the raised leg which Bottom holds. At the same time Topman jumps, Bottom lifts with all his might and through a distance of three or four feet (Fig. 2). This gives Topman an extended take-off and throws him high into the air. He should go up nearly ten feet.

Topman must be careful not to tuck until he has reached the peak of his jump and then to break tuck quickly in order to float down easily and keep from going over too far (Figs. 3 and 4).

1. *2.* *3.* *4.*

When Bottom receives the kick from the throw-foot at the take-off he must not sag or "give." The dip is as much "giving" as he is allowed. His throw must be long and straight up. The follow-through is important and should be carried above the shoulders. He pushes with his legs as well as with his arms. His torso is vertical throughout; his head up and chin held in. Topman need not be frightened by the extreme height of this throw. So long as he has control of his body he can somersault just as easily high as low. But he must keep his eyes open; he is way up in the air.

When first practicing this stunt do not throw full height. It is very simple when the throw is low. You may increase the force of the throw as you become more confident and better controlled. It is a beautiful performance when full height is attained.

Variations:

Pitchback with a lay-out.

Pitchback with a half-twist.

Pitchback with a full-twist.

(Others to be described in detail later.)

DOUBLE FLIP

The two partners stand facing each other about two feet apart. Each leans over obliquely to the right and forward, raising his left arm above his head. They embrace each other's waists, and Bottom lifts Topman off the mat (Fig. 1) to a vertical position in which there are feet on both ends (Fig. 2). The head of each is between the legs of the other at the crotch, not at the knees. The embrace is tight so the pair may act as a single figure.

Bottom leans back, bending at the knees and arching his back greatly. This brings Topman's feet to the mats (Fig. 3). Topman then lifts Bottom to the vertical position, and the tide is turned. Topman, now, leans back and allows Bottom to stand once more.   So the flip goes, end over end.

You will find it easier to place one foot slightly ahead of the other, and to flip the back leg a little before the forward one.   The stunt is more pleasing, though a little more difficult, if each man takes one step forward (opposite to the direction of progression) as he comes onto his feet.   This takes up less room too, which is another advantage.

1.   *2.*   *3.*   *4.*

It is difficult to end this stunt.   Stop in Position 3. Topman takes his arms from around his partner's waist, and putting his hands on Bottom's shoulder, shoves him forward and up.   Bottom releases his grip when he receives this shove and comes to a stand (Fig. 4).

Make your turns in good rhythm.   When you become proficient, you can flip very quickly and with a sharp whip as in flip-flops.   It is even possible to end the stunt by having Bottom throw Topman, from the position of Figure 1, over his head onto Topman's feet.   The grips, of course, must be released on the throw.   This is very difficult to do, and requires good momentum from the preceding flips.   It is also a strain on backs, if care is not exercised.   Take it easy.   Do not try this finish until you are confident you can handle it.

Hand-to-hand Balance

The field of hand-to-hand balancing is quite extensive—and a field for the specialist.   Usually tumblers do very little of this work, and conversely, balancers do little ground tumbling.   Here we shall describe only the simplest things in hand-to-hand balancing.

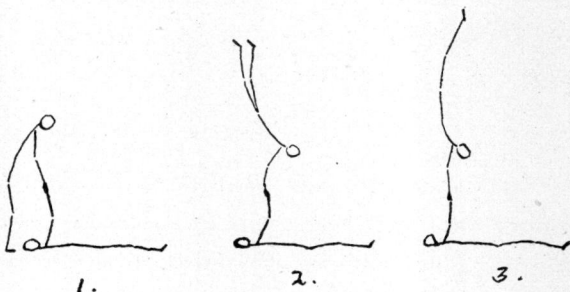

1.   2.   3.

Bottom lies on his back, legs extended, arms raised. Topman stands at his shoulders, facing his feet.   The grip is: palms together, thumbs interlocked, fingers spread.   The wrists of each man are bent back slightly and the fingers grip tightly (Fig. 1).

Topman throws into place by leaning forward on the arms, and flipping his body up into position with one quick throw.   One leg goes ahead of the other (Figs. 1, 2, and 3).

After the throw both men's arms must be held stiff. Topman is locked rigidly. The few movements he makes are with his wrists. Bottom does most of the balancing.

To finish the stunt Topman falls back to starting position; or he may swing his legs through Bottom's arms and come to a stand between Bottom's spread legs, where he can pull up and forward, lifting Bottom to his feet.

Good balancers may try several interesting variations:

Push up to handstand from swinging position.

Push up from same position, Bottom standing.

Pull up, as in pull-up mount (p. 118), to handstand.

High Shoulder Stand

The partners stand facing each other with arms gripped as for the teeter-totter, and the low shoulder stand. Topman jumps up to a straddle of Bottom's chest (Fig. 1). Bottom bends forward—only a little—as a wind-up (Fig. 2), and throws vigorously back toward the upright position, lifting with his arms at the same time. Topman releases his legs and swings up above Bottom's shoulders. He goes up in a half-tuck position, his hips leading (Fig. 3). As soon as he is up, he straightens—or more accurately—arches to the shoulder stand (Fig. 4). Topman's arms are on the outside from start to stand. In the last position his weight is very lightly overbalanced backwards and he maintains equilibrium by clamping his hands tightly against Bottom's biceps just below the elbow. He must grip with thumb and fingers just as in the low shoulder stand.

The throw is not difficult once you get the trick of it, but it calls for close cooperation. Let Topman remember to jump up high under the arms at the start, and not to extend the hips until he is well above Bottom's shoulders on the throw. Bottom may take as many steps as necessary to gain or maintain balance—the fewer, the better.

SLIDE

Topman stands with legs apart. Bottom, approaching from the rear, bends over, and puts his head between the legs of Topman, as in the neckbreaker. Instead of throwing from this position he merely straightens up to a stand with Topman sitting astride his neck. Bending at the knees and hips slightly, he leans for-

Before the throw for high shoulders stand.

ward, allowing Topman to slide backward a little, preliminary to the full slide (Fig. 1).

Topman straightens his legs and bends as sharply as he can at the hips. He holds on to Bottom with his hands beneath Bottom's armpits. He starts to slide slowly, then goes faster as he drops. He holds himself to his partner with his hands which slide down Bottom's sides (Fig. 2). When they reach Bottom's hips, they

1.   2.   3.   4.   5.

stop, and Topman in a sort of tuck position swings through Bottom's legs (Fig. 3). Bottom catches Topman by the hips immediately from the front and pulls him through the legs onto his feet (Figs. 4 and 5). The stunt must be perfectly timed. Bottom is almost vertical at the start of the slide. He leans forward more as Topman gets going. Topman holds on just long enough to cause him to swing through his partner's legs. Bottom must catch him and support him from then on. Topman must keep well bent over throughout the stunt. Especially must he be tucked close as he goes through the wicket (see diagram).

Bottom may have difficulty getting the proper inclination of his back; and Topman, sliding and holding on at once.   Experiment a bit with these problems.

When you have practiced considerably you will be able to slide with zip.   It's a nice stunt, and usually gives the spectators a laugh.

SLING

This stunt is for partners of unequal size.   Bottom puts his left arm beneath both Topman's arms and

1.   *2.*   *3.*   *4.*   *5.*

behind his back.   He then drapes Topman across his own back, holding Topman's legs with his right arm behind their knees, as in the saddle-back carry (Fig. 1). Topman's belly is against Bottom's back, and his whole figure clamped to Bottom's back by means of the latter's arms passing behind his thorax and knees.

Bottom begins the throw by twisting a little to the right as a wind-up.   Then releasing Topman's head-end, he slings forcibly to the left pulling hard on his right arm which is hooked with Topman's bent knees. Topman swings out behind and around counter-clock-wise, hanging only by his knees (Fig. 2).   Bottom catches his head-end as it swings around in front, and holds Topman as a child in arms (Fig. 3). Bottom then drops Topman's legs, and holding him around the thorax with his own left arm, slings him around behind (Fig. 3). As the legs come up across Bottom's back, he hooks his right arm behind the knees and holds them as before (Fig. 5). This is repeated several times.

You will find it necessary to balk, and twist in the opposite direction for a wind-up, between slings, in front and in back. When the slings come rapidly this is an impressive stunt. Topman seems to be getting rough treatment; but it should not hurt him in the least. Be sure that you have plenty of room when you begin to sling, and be careful of your balance.

THREE JUMPS TO SHOULDERS

Bottom gets down on all fours, back to the mat as in the crab walk. Topman stands on his belly (Fig. 1). At the proper signal, Topman jumps straight up, and during the moment he is in the air Bottom turns over face down, on all fours still. Topman alights on his back (Fig. 3). Topman then makes a second jump, straight up, and Bottom gets onto his feet with his hips sticking well out behind for Topman to alight on (Fig. 3). Topman makes the third jump, from Bottom's hips to his shoulders, the latter straightening up to full stand during the interval. Bottom must

12

grasp Topman's calves and clamp the junction for a regular two-high stand, in addition to balancing the whole structure. He may take as many steps as are necessary.

Bottom must change positions very quickly and accurately. Topman must jump high and do some delicate balancing. He uses his arms to help. Both must understand exactly where the other will be after

each jump, and behave accordingly. It is not as easy as it may seem on first consideration, but it is fun and gets your interest.

FRONT OR BACK SOMERSAULT FROM A BASKET

Make a basket by grasping with your right hand your own left wrist, and by grasping with your left hand your partner's right wrist (Fig. 1).

A third man now mounts to a standing position on the hands (Fig. 2). He may balance himself getting into position by putting his hand on his partners' heads. From this position he jumps front or back for a front or back somersault. The bottom men aid him in the throw by pulling back and up on the arms (Fig. 3). They afford a pretty good force. The starting position is precarious. Be careful to have perfect balance at the take-off, otherwise you will not have good control in the air. The somersault technics are very nearly the same as from a stand on the mats, except that the

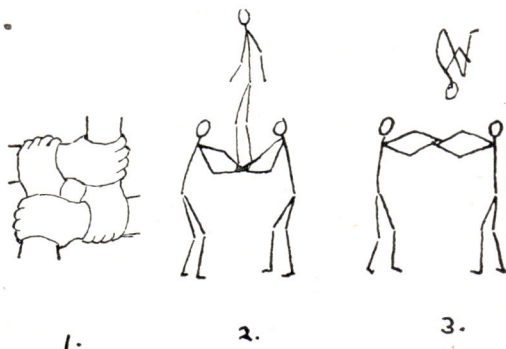

1.   2.   3.

take-off is slower and longer. The height is greater, too, so break your tuck early and be careful not to go over too far. The bottom men can catch Topman if he loses control. Everyone must watch every move closely.

Front Somersault through Legs

Bottom stands on his head in the middle of the mats, with his legs widespread, stiff, and toes pointed. Topman runs in from the direction of his back, and takes-off for a front somersault from a point two feet from

Bottom's head.   Topman must get a tremendous jump
and go high enough to turn his somersault between
Bottom's legs without touching him.   The tendency is
for Topman to go over too far on coming out of the
somersault, so he will find it convenient to take a simple
roll immediately on alighting.   This stunt is very
spectacular, and surprisingly easy to tumblers with
good jumping legs.   Be careful not to take-off too far

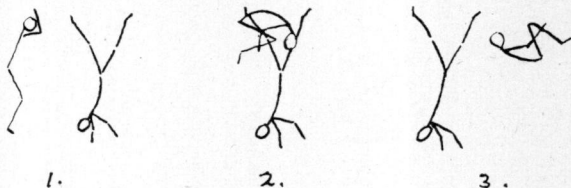

away from the underman, and to get your height before
you tuck.   Bottom does well to assume a slanting
position, as in the diagram, so that if he gets hit, his
head won't be driven straight into the floor.   A light
blow will not hurt either party.

FRONT FROM FOREARMS

Topman mounts for two-high position.   Bottom
grips his own right wrist with left hand and holds his
arms up in front of and close to his chest.   Topman
steps on the forearms resting his heels on the upper
arm for balance (Fig. 1).

At the proper signal Topman leaps into a front
somersault.   Bottom throws with his arm—and also

with his legs—at the moment Topman jumps, thus
aiding him on the take-off. Technics for making the
somersault are like those for standing front, but the
take-off is slower and longer, and the tuck must be
broken sooner. Take care to watch for the ceiling as

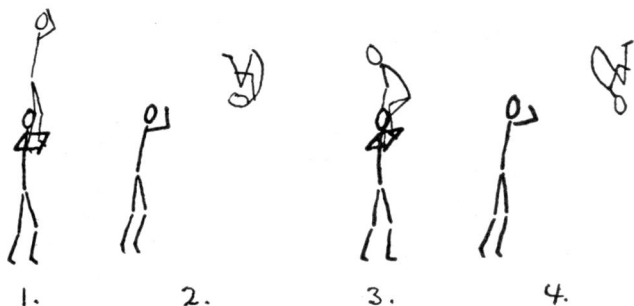

1.   2.   3.   4.

you go over. Bottom must follow-through on the arm
throw.

BACK FROM FOREARMS

[See illustration above]

Topman stands on the forearms of his partner as in
the last stunt but facing the opposite direction. He
may get to this position from the regular two-high or
may mount from the floor, having Bottom kneel on
one leg for the purpose. During the mount and preliminary to jumping he may keep balance by holding
onto Bottom's head (Fig. 3). Before jumping, of
course, he must stand erect. The back somersault technic is regular. Since there is a throw from the arms on

which he stands, the take-off must be slower and longer.
Because of the height break tuck early. Watch for
the floor while you are turning. Bottom performs as
in the last stunt.

Front from Thighs

Topman mounts to Bottom's thighs as for planché,
then assumes position for standing front somersault.
Bottom grasps his shins and thereby holds him in place

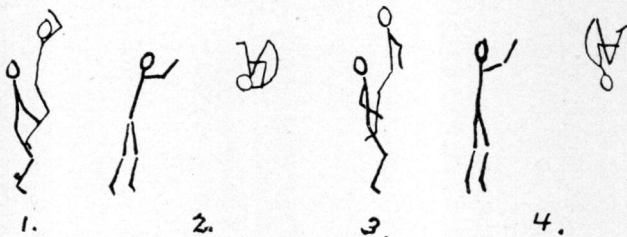

1.   2.   3.   4.

(Fig. 1). At the signal Topman jumps as he would for
standing front somersault. Bottom lifts with his arms
and pushes out, spinning Topman nicely. As soon as
Topman's feet have left Bottom's thighs Bottom pushes
with his legs as well.

If you would like to try a fancier mount, have Bottom
stand just behind Topman with hands on Topman's
waist, and Topman grasping his wrists. At the first
signal Topman jumps straight up and Bottom lifts to
aid him. Bottom's hands are quickly shifted to Topman's shins, and the latter alights in place on Bottom's
thighs. Without a halt, Topman winds up and throws

for the somersault.   This looks pretty snappy.   You must be careful of your balance.   Try the mount and the somersault separately at first, then put them together without the balk in between.

Back from Thighs

Bottom stands as for planché.   Topman steps into place, putting his hands on Bottom's shoulders for balance.   Topman's feet are turned out so that they rest obliquely across Bottom's thighs near the hip joints.   Topman stands and throws first as he would for standing back somersault from the floor.   Bottom gives the same kind of throw described in the last stunt.   This is easier than the front from thighs.

You can also mount with the jump, as for the front.   Because the feet are turned out you may find it hard to take-off for the somersault.   A little practice will accustom you to the position.

Front or Back from Hips

Bottom stoops over with hands on knees, back slightly curved, but approximately horizontal.   Topman stands on Bottom's hips, facing the opposite direction (Fig. 1).   At the signal Topman takes-off for the front somersault, getting a tremendous boost from Bottom, who pushes up sharply with legs and arms somewhat as in the kip-from-back (Fig. 2).   The take-off is slightly slower than in a front from the floor;

and because of the height be careful when you open tuck.

Instructions are practically the same for the back from hips. The only differences are in the direction Topman faces at the start, and the usual differences in technics of front and back somersault, which you should know perfectly by now.

1.   2.   3.   4.   5.

Another way to mount is to have Topman lie on his belly (for the front somersault) on the mats, and Bottom back up between his legs. Bottom picks up Topman (whose body is stiff) by the ankles and puts his hips beneath Topman's crotch (Fig. 4). He then leans forward and presses down on the back of Topman's ankles which brings Topman up to a sitting position astride Bottom's back (Fig. 5), from which he goes to the stand for the somersault.

This may be done for the back somersault as well. In the beginning Topman lies on his back instead of his belly.

For the front somersault a take-off can be made from sitting position on Bottom's back, thereby eliminating one movement, the stand. To throw a somersault from sitting position rise on the legs as the arms go above the shoulders in the wind-up.

Run-up Mount

Bottom stoops over, hands on knees, legs well braced, and hips sticking out behind as in third position of three-jumps-to-shoulder (Fig. 1).

1.   2.   3.   4.

Topman runs in and leaps from his right foot, about 24 inches from Bottom. The left foot is placed on Bottom's left hip for the first step (Fig. 2), the right foot is placed on Bottom's right shoulder for the second step (Fig. 3), and the left foot is then brought up onto the left shoulder for the last step (Fig. 4). Bottom straightens up as soon as the left foot is removed from his hip, and grasps his partner's calves to clamp the junction for two-high position.

It is difficult to have the proper balance throughout this stunt. Topman must jump high and almost straight up when he leaves the ground. Bottom must

brace against being kicked forward. As soon as Topman reaches the shoulders, Bottom tries to balance
him. This is not easy, and unless Topman is an
accurate jumper Bottom will have to take a few steps.
Even then he may not be sure of balance. Topman's
arms can aid in gaining balance.

HIGH BACK SOMERSAULT

This is a back somersault from Bottom's shoulders,
two-high position. Topman stands on his instep, toes

1.   2.   3.   4.   5.

pointing slightly down, knees bent a little, body erect
(Fig. 1). His wind-up for the back somersault is
exactly the same as on the floor. Bottom stands
almost rigid, a little bend and a little spring in his
legs (Fig. 2). As Topman takes-off Bottom does not
recoil but gives a short quick push with his legs and
toes, at the same time he pushes up with his arms on

High back somersault.

Topman's legs (Fig. 3). Topman flies high, does a quick tuck, opens early, and floats down fully out-stretched (Figs. 4 and 5).

Topman's jump must be nearly straight up. Bottom must watch him during flight and step forward if necessary to get out of his way. He is also ready to catch Topman in case Topman should lose control, which he had better not do. Bottom must bend very little with his knees; nevertheless, throw hard on the take-off, *and in time*. Practice the jump alone until you are sure of it.

This is a magnificent stunt when done with precision and force. Be careful.

High Front Somersault

This is not very different from the high back. It is a little more difficult, however. You must be sure of your balance, sure of coordination, and understand definitely the throw. Bottom behaves exactly as in the last stunt, except that he leans forward a little on the throw (Fig. 3). Topman's take-off is the same except that it is for front somersault instead of back. If you are sure of each other and can depend on being together for the throw, the rest of the stunt is easy. Topman, of course, must watch for the ceiling when he turns, and break tuck soon. It is necessary that Topman have good control of himself in the air, because of the great height to which he goes, and because it is not easy for him to see where he is going. This is a comparatively dangerous stunt. Use the belt while learning.

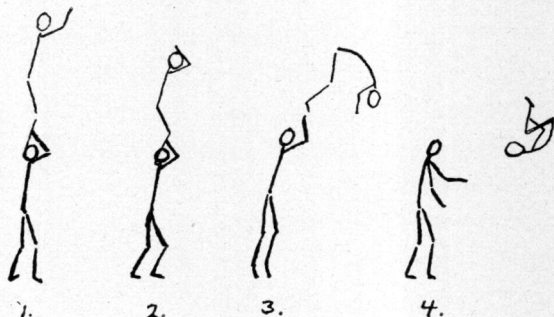

1.   2.   3.   4.

Running Front Overhead

This is like the pitchback except that Topman is thrown up, completely over Bottom, and turns a front somersault in the bargain (see diagram).

1.   2.   3.   4.

Bottom stands with feet apart, knees bent, trunk erect, arms placed as for pitchback. Topman runs in,

places his hands on Bottom's shoulders and one foot
in the pocket of Bottom's hands (Fig. 1). The pair
dips for the wind-up only a little. Then Topman
jumps quickly and hard, up and slightly forward. His
arms are slung up as he jumps, and Bottom throws
vigorously at the same time (Fig. 2). When Topman
reaches the peak of his jump he tucks, throwing down
forcibly with his arms, rounding shoulders, etc. (Fig.
3). If he is not in the right position, and has not the
right inclination of his body at the time of the tuck
he will have difficulty getting his spin. The force for
the spin must come from tucking, not from the take-off.
This means that the take-off must be exactly right.
All these high fronts call for delicate control at the
take-off and while in the air. They must not be
attempted until you have practiced the throws, separately, enough to be sure of them.

Topman watches for the ceiling and breaks tuck
early here as before (Fig. 4). Bottom should be
ready to catch Topman in case he blunders.

Running Front from Back

This stunt is first cousin to the standing front from
back described earlier. Bottom stoops over with hands
on knees, legs apart and well braced. His back is
slightly curved, but approximately horizontal. His
elbows and knees are bent, ready for a good push
upward. Bottom runs in from the front, pounces—

very much as in the regular take-off from two feet—onto
the middle of Bottom's back (Figs. 1 and 2). From
there he jumps immediately for the front somersault.
Bottom pushes up as he jumps, giving a big
boost, as in the standing front from back (Fig. 3).
Bottom must not sag much with the impact of
Topman's pounce. The technic for the somersault is
regular.

1.   2.   3.   4.

Important points regarding the performance of this
stunt are accuracy and cooperation, just as is the case
with all of the last four stunts described.

Handstand and Double Over

Topman does a handstand at his partner's heels,
dropping his feet over Bottom's shoulders, exactly as in
the handstand roll. Bottom grasps the ankles firmly
(Fig. 1).

To throw, Bottom bends forward, at the same time
pulling down on Topman's legs. Topman draws
himself up, bending at the hips, but keeping his back

straight (Fig. 2).   He makes this upward swing in such a way as to get considerable momentum for flying over the top of Bottom's shoulders (Fig. 3).   As he goes over the top.   Bottom pushes up on the legs, which helps Topman fly into the air for a front somersault (Figs. 3 and 4).   To understand better the method in which Topman is thrown, imagine that Bottom has a hoe-handle over his shoulder in place of Topman.   When he pulls down on the butt end, the pole acts as a lever.

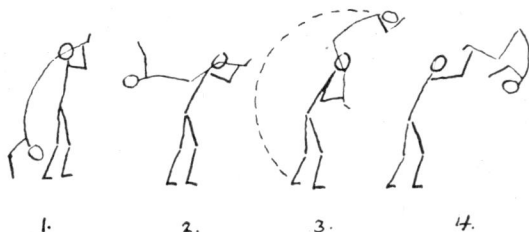

1.   2.   3.   4.

The long end flips over his shoulder with great speed and if the butt end is shoved up at the right moment, the pole may be thrown for some distance.   Topman is better than a stiff pole.   He can aid in the throw.   By drawing up against the downward pull which Bottom exerts, he increases the force by which he is thrown. During the swing Topman must not round his back and thereby bring his head and shoulders closer to Bottom. Doing so would reduce the leverage, reduce the arc through which his head and shoulders swing, and consequently reduce the speed and force with which the forepart of his body travels.

13

Since in this stunt Topman begins with a handstand, and ends standing upright, it is a one-and-a-half somersault.   Hence the name.

The most important part of this stunt is learning to make the most of the swing up from the handstand. Study the diagram.   You will find the belt helpful in learning.

CHAPTER XI

ADAPTATION

Tumbling for Youngsters

It is a peculiar fact that the younger a person is the quicker he learns tumbling. It is no job at all to teach a two-year-old to do the roll. Sometimes it is quite a task to teach his father. Many of the best tumblers in the country are youths in their teens.

It has been mentioned earlier that this sport is very near to our animal instincts for play. These instincts are stronger in children, and are more freely expressed. Practically all youngsters take to tumbling readily. And if they have the proper instruction to enable them to really make headway at learning stunts, they become very interested indeed. Tumbling seems to be more appreciated in the elementary and junior high schools than anywhere else. Those who gain unusual skill at performing, are anxious to carry on in high school and college. When they start young, and have adequate instruction, they learn a surprising lot in two or three years of practice. Also, the activity means a great deal of pleasure, and results in very desirable physiological outcomes.

Tumbling for youngsters should be well supervised. Boys especially, have admirable courage and are not afraid to try anything. However, if left to themselves, they do not always take the proper precautions. An adult standing by as a spotter can be very helpful. Children's bodies are light and in case of accident can be caught or spun easily. Whenever difficult stunts are being tried someone should be on hand to do this. Because they are small, children have less distance to fall and hit with less impact. Also they are more flexible than adults, and usually know better how to fall. So, if you have mats, belt, and proper supervision, there is very little danger and plenty of fun.

The order of stunts in this book is suitable for youngsters as well as for others. Perhaps they will not be able to progress as far as older and more experienced persons, but so long as they are properly supervised they may go as far as their capabilities permit. It will not hurt them to do the most advanced stunts, provided they know the technics and appreciate the need for being careful.

It is surprising what a good program can be put on using only the simplest stunts—nothing more difficult than a handspring. We must remember that a display should not be merely the attempt to do difficult stunts. Rather it should be the attempt to do things which are beautiful. The simplest movements, when made gracefully, are interesting and pleasing.

An adult performer and a youngster, working together, make an interesting team. The great difference in sizes makes possible a large variety of stunts. It also makes possible varying specific stunts in many different ways. Sometimes in school shows, if the instructor and one of the small boys will work together, they can contribute considerable of the spectacular to the program.

TUMBLING FOR GIRLS

It is customary for parents to shelter and protect their girls from the little hardships of life, and at the same time require that their boys meet these very hardships as a part of life's training. Boys are usually given a great deal of freedom; and girls, very little. Too often the path of life is prepared for the girl, instead of the girl for the path of life.

It is just as *natural* for girls to romp, and climb and do boyish stunts as for their brothers—only it isn't *customary*. Up to the beginning of puberty their bodies are as well suited to all sorts of physical activity as are the boys'. Tumbling is a good vigorous sport for young girls, and they like it fully as well as do the boys.

No differentiation of the program is required for girls up to about the age of twelve. For girls beyond that age the program must be adapted to their physical differences. The most important of these are broader pelvis; relatively weaker arms, shoulder, and trunk muscles; and more delicate internal organic systems. The broadened pelvis interferes with facility in running and jumping. It means also more difficulty in balance. Weaker arms, shoulder, and trunk muscles will eliminate from the program all stunts which call for strong exertion by the upper parts of the body. Because of delicate internal organic systems older girls should not perform stunts which involve great and sudden expenditures of effort, heavy jolts, or strains in lifting. This eliminates nearly all the stunts in the section for experts and many of the stunts in the section on advanced tumbling.

On the other hand girls are more limber than boys, and can do better a great many stunts calling for flexibility rather than strength. There is much controversy at present about the advisability of extreme back bending. We do not recommend it.

Girls tend to make more of the aesthetics in tumbling than do boys. They can devote more attention to the beauty of lines and grouping. The elementary stunts lend themselves very well to creative work in this direction. Combinations of tumbling and the dance are extremely good, and offer opportunities for the display of real talent.

Despite the fact that the number of stunts in which girls can participate is limited, tumbling for them can be just as interesting and worthwhile as for the boys.

A pyramid by girls.

CHAPTER XII

THE SHOW

ONE of the recognized values of sports is the innocent pleasure they afford performers through a modest display of superiority, whatever its nature. The desire to excel is a fine spur to action, and in itself, is a good influence. Vanity is considered bad more often than good. This kind of vanity, however, is certainly harmless, and still plays a large part in every branch of our sport life. Those who spend time and effort developing a special skill or talent like to show it. What's more, they like to have it appreciated, which is only right.

In the highly competitive sports, to do well at the game, or meet, is the object of training. Each sportsman, or team wants to show an objective superiority over his or its, opponent. In the display sports objective measurement is impossible. Nevertheless, a superior performance can be readily recognized, and should be as readily appreciated by spectators as victory in race or game. Applause of the audience is to the display performer what victory is to the contestant.

The emotions which attend each specific success act as an impetus to further improvement, and lend to work and practice a joy and encouragement.

Shows and display performances are an integral part of tumbling work, and can afford a lot of fun. A good display, however, involves more than tumbling skill, and more than fun. It requires showmanship. Certain elements are common to all good shows, regardless of types. They are: nice design, rhythmic movement, and unusual materials. Anyone who has read the foregoing pages cannot fail to appreciate the opportunities in tumbling for display work. In an earlier chapter it was said that "Human beings can be arranged in groups as lovely as any painted design, with the added grace of movement." This is a striking truth. A wide variety of space and time rhythms have been herein suggested. Materials, both easy and difficult, which are unusual and interesting have been set forth in detail. This is stuff in abundance from which to make your show.

Answers to the question what shall we include in the program? must of course be conditioned by the purpose of the show, the character of the audience, and the degree of skill possessed by the performers. Usually a tumbling display is one act among several. Brevity is a distinct asset. You will find that although people universally are interested in stunts, their interest is good for short periods only. Fifteen minutes should be

Small group pyramids.

Note the use of curved lines.

a maximum length for the ordinary act. Ten minutes is usually long enough. It is surprising how much can be crammed into ten minutes of fast tumbling; and better too little than too much. One remembers more pleasantly a good meal of which there was not enough, than one of which there was more than enough. So with the tumbling act. Make your performance flashy, and leave the audience "hungry."

The program of stunts should be well organized. It should be arranged so as to produce best effect for the audience, and to allow most comfort for the performers. The problem is more difficult than it seems. You must allow individual performers a proper rest after each series of stunts, and alternate performances so as not to over-tax any individual or pair. At the same time your act must build to a climax and be made as dramatic as possible.

You will find it convenient to line up stunts in *combinations* or *series*, which allow smooth transition from one to another and break up the act into convenient units of performance. For example, one series for a pair of workers may be: *Cross dives—pitchback—belly pitch—chute pick-up.* To perform this series, the two men enter by running in from opposite sides, and diving so as to cross each other in flight at center stage. On alighting, they roll, get to their feet, and turn to face each other. A takes stance as understander for pitchback, and B runs in to be thrown.

After pitching B, A does a single roll and gets on his back into position to throw B for belly pitch. On alighting from the belly pitch, B turns, walks into A, who is still on his back, takes A's hands, and throws him for chute pick-up. They exit together, immediately after this final throw.

An act may be composed of five or ten short series. It is a good idea to alternate companion series with individual stunts or combinations. Each man has a chance to rest while someone else is performing. You will find it takes considerable manipulating, especially where there are but two performers, to arrange the program so that every man will be able to last throughout the act, and so there will be no break in the sequence.

In any particular program the list of series or stunts will depend upon the build and skill of the particular performers. If, for example, the pair in the foregoing paragraph were so different in size that B couldn't throw A for chute pick-up, the series could not be used without alteration. It is a good idea to make a list beforehand of all the stunts your group can do. Then go to the gymnasium with pencil and paper, and figure out your program. Try various combinations of stunts, and see how they fit together. It is necessary, in large part, to determine the arrangement by trial and error.

Following are suggested programs, for pairs, from each of the three main sections of the book.

ELEMENTARY

1. Continuous backward rolls (A and B from opposite
      sides to center)
    Snap-ups
    Knee roll
    A—headstand (with legs spread)
    B—dive (over A)
2. Forward double roll (across stage)
    Backward double roll (return)
    Ankle pick-up
    Teeter-totter
3. A—continuous cartwheels
    B—handspring
4. Elephant walk (across stage)
    Camel walk (return)
5. Straddle, front and back
    Planché
    Step-mount (walk around stage, two-high)
    Fall forward and rolls.

ADVANCED

1. Shoulder stand, shift, down and up (turn to stand
      facing)
    Pull-up mount
    Down and over
2. A—cartwheels with jumps
    B—fall forward to handstand
    A—high kick and slap
    14

3. One leg back
   Elbow pitch
   Kip off back
   B—egg roll
   Roll up and somersault
4. High roll
5. B—front somersault
   A—Dive handspring (over B)
   Seat pitch
   Belly pitch
6. B—buck
   A—back handsprings
7. Bird lift (end with throw and roll)
   Neckbreaker
   One leg front
   Straddle pitch
   Chute pick-up

Expert

1. A—round-off, side somersault
   B—round-off, back handspring, back somersault
   A—round-off, back somersault with half-twist
   B—round-off, back layout somersault
2. Run-up mount (walk around stage, two-high)
   High back somersault
   Pitchback
   Sling

3. Shoulder stand, shift, down and up (B stands and shifts, A comes up)

   High shoulder stand (fall over to feet)

4. B—gainer

   A—tinsica, front somersault

5. Three jumps to shoulders

   Slide

6. A—back handsprings with half-twist

   B—cradle

   A—Standing front somersault

   B—Front layout somersault

7. High roll (across stage)

   Double flip, end with throw (return)

Tumbling by pairs seems to be the most popular type of performance. Of course there are many other types. Some have a story or plot, are a kind of romantic pantomime, (*e. g.*, a picture of the Olympiad, or Punch and Judy). Some are merely slap-stick, (*e. g.*, clown show). Others are highly intermixed with music and dance. The opportunity for variety is infinite. It offers an attractive challenge to your imagination and creative ability.

Historically, the tumbler is a clown. You will find it a good suggestion to make your act lively with comedy. Stunts like the egg-roll and the high kick lend themselves readily to monkey-business. Many other stunts when slightly changed become very funny. You can have a grand time figuring out such changes. People who may care little for a difficult performance will sometimes be delighted by the merriment of comedy stunts. Everyone likes to laugh. And laughter mixes well with tumbling.

Costumes and stage setting will of course depend on the nature of your act. We can, however, formulate a few rules which apply generally. 1. The less equipment you can safely do with, the better. 2. Let the color of your costumes contrast with the background of the stage set. 3. Be careful to select costumes which will not impede your movements. 4. Have costumes fastened on securely so they wont come off during the show. About half the amateur performances are held up temporarily by such accidents. 5. Consider together the stage, your intended act, and the expected audience when you decide upon settings and costumes. (Note Frontispiece.)

It's heaps of fun putting on a show. Try it.

BIBLIOGRAPHY

Butterworth, H., *How To*, published privately 1899.

Cotteral, B. and D., *Tumbling Pyramid Building and Stunts*, A. S. Barnes, N. Y., 1926.

Dewey, John, *Democracy and Education*, Macmillan, N. Y., 1916.

Good, C. V., *How To Do Research in Education*, Warwick, Baltimore, 1929.

Gwathmey, J. T., *Tumbling for Amateurs*, Am. Sports Pub. Co., N. Y., 1927.

H'Doubler, M. N., *The Dance and Its Place in Education*, Harcourt, Brace, N. Y., 1925.

McClow and Anderson, *Tumbling Illustrated*, A. S. Barnes, N. Y., 1931.

Pearl, N. H. and Brown, H. E., *Health by Stunts*, Macmillan, N. Y., 1926.

Rodgers, M., *Handbook of Stunts*, Macmillan, N. Y., 1928.

Williams, J. F., *Principles of Physical Education*, W. B. Saunders Co., Philadelphia, 1930.

Williams, J. F., *Personal Hygiene Applied*, W. B. Saunders Co., Philadelphia, 1931.

Worth, H. W., *Ground Tumbling*, Am. Sports Pub. Co., N. Y., 1927.

The Eurhythmics of Jacques-Dalcrose, Small Maynard, Boston, 1928.

213

INDEX OF STUNTS

215